THE LAND OF UNLIKENESS

Keeping faith for a new century

Nigel Collinson

I think there are good reasons for suggesting that the modern age has ended. Today, many things indicate that we are going through a transitional period, when it seems that something is on the way out and something else is painfully being born. It is as if something were crumbling, decaying and exhausting itself, while something else, still indistinct, were arising from the rubble.

Václav Havel
Philadelphia, 4th July 1994

ISBN 1 85852 075 4

© Nigel Collinson 1996
Foundery Press

Cover: *The Creation Embroidery* by Angela Dewar and Gisela Banbury.
Salisbury Methodist Church. Photograph by David Grinter.

Printed in England by Clays Ltd, St Ives plc.

He is the Way.
Follow him through the Land of Unlikeness;
You will see rare beasts, and have unique adventures.

He is the Truth.
Seek him in the Kingdom of Anxiety;
You will come to a great city that has expected your
return for years.

He is the Life.
Love him in the World of the Flesh;
And at your marriage all its occasions shall dance for joy.

W. H. Auden
from *Flight into Egypt*

CONTENTS

Introduction   1

1. The Twentieth Century – Another Look   3

    1. A changed landscape   3
    2. 'While we range with science'   4
    3. 'Into the melting'   6
    4. Theology for the Third Millennium   10

2. End of Century   14

    1. The way things work   17
    2. Time and space   20
    3. How we organize ourselves   22
    4. The way we are now   25

3. Future Choices   29

    1. The End of History . . . ?   29
    2. The Postmodern Turn   31
    3. The 'Me' Generation   34
    4. Fundamentalism   36
    5. Making choices   37
    6. A critical, contemporary Christianity   39

4. Conversation   43

    1. A network of conversations   43
    2. A theology at ease with itself   46
    3. In the Land of Unlikeness   48
    4. Relative Adequacy or Modest Faithfulness?   50

5. Are we getting ahead of God?   53

    1. Wonder and unbelief   53
    2. The man in green trousers   55
    3. Porous world   56
    4. Origins   58
    5. Are we getting ahead of God?   64

6. 'Nothing Is Beyond Redemption'   67

    1.   Recognition and hope   67
    2.   Recapitulation   71
    3.   Redemptive Suffering   73
    4.   Redemptive obedience   75
    5.   Summing things up   77

7. In the Land of Unlikeness   80

    1.   In the Land of Unlikeness   80
    2.   A generation of surfers   83
    3.   A common place   86
    4.   A church of the common place   90
    5.   A highway shall be there   94

Notes   99

INTRODUCTION

'There's something happening out there, don't you think?' someone said to me about half a dozen years ago at the end of the Eighties. Since then I've pressed him several times to expand on what he said. It has continued to echo around. Although the signs were there through the 1980s that something was happening, it is only now that we can begin to appreciate just how significant that change has become. It is not a question of politics and economics alone; something underlying it all has shifted. We are in a different place, culturally, from even ten years ago. This is affecting deeply the way we see the world, the ability of the Christian Church to connect with people's lives and the shape of what I shall call 'our keeping faith'.

What follows is by way of a conversation in which you will have your own ideas, your own background, your own visions. Some people will have other views, some will want to take another look and perhaps a few will say, 'Yes, that's what I think too, but I wouldn't put it quite like that.' That's in the nature of a conversation, where we share our viewpoints, agreeing and disagreeing. The main thing is that the conversation continues.

First of all, *The Land of Unlikeness* tries to position us at the turn of the century, looking backwards along the way we have come, but then, in chapter two, taking what might seem an unusual look at the new landscape. There is debate about where we are in our cultural history at the present moment. Chapter three seeks to describe that debate and to make a proposal. Chapter four is about a way of doing our thinking, making our important decisions, keeping faith with our ideals and the springs of our inspiration, which is all about conversation.

No faith which seeks to make a contribution to the great debates of our times can by-pass the need for credibility. Although such knowing is not always at the forefront of our minds, we do need to know that in the end Christianity is defensible in the light of all that is going on in the world in this latter part of the twentieth century. Chapter five makes a very tentative contribution to that discussion. John F. Haught's book, *Science and Religion*,[1] came too late for me to make use of it, although I noted the sub-title, 'From conflict to conversation'. Long live healthy, robust conversation!

The twentieth century has seen conflict and cruelty on a grand scale and many people come to the end of a decade and of a century with a burdened, anxious feeling as well as a sense of optimism. Keeping faith needs also to deal with our mixed emotions and with the scars on our humanity. Chapter six, therefore, tries to interpret what redemption means, first of all in contemporary films and literature and then in sacrifice and in obedient lives, in which our century has not been lacking despite all. The great themes of creation and redemption are important, however, because they are central to the Christian vision. They express our core belief that this is God's world and that applies whether we are talking the language of the Bible or the language of late twentieth century novels or films. They give us a way of handling life in all its strange complexity. The final chapter, therefore, uses the image of the surfer to find a way into some of the challenges that now face us. Its main lines were sketched out some time before I read the first sentence of Richard Hoggart's *The Way We Live Now*.[2]

I am grateful to a number of people who have read drafts of all or part of the text and who have suggested corrections and offered new and better ideas – Alan Grist, John Ogden, Ray and Kath Short, Peter Evans, Bill Patton, Derek Long, Colin Scarrett and Brenda Beamond. I also need to thank the staff of Sarum College Library in Salisbury for their help. Thank you to Salisbury Methodist Church and to David Grinter for allowing me to use *The Creation Embroidery* on the cover. Several years ago I had a series of conversations with Professor Mary Grey and Dr. Joseph Cassidy at La Sainte Union College in Southampton and I am immensely grateful to them. The Editorial Panel of the Epworth Press gave the book its very patient consideration; I am greatly indebted to Susan Hibbins and Sue Gascoigne of the Methodist Publishing House and to Brian Thornton who gave the go-ahead to publish it. I hope the book is worthy of all their hard work. Writing is sometimes a lonely business, especially when it is not going particularly well, so I must express my thanks to Lorna for her constant encouragement. Finally, I recall the people with whom I have shared conversations around countless meal tables, in retreats and conferences, after sermons and addresses in churches large and small, in the Southampton District and beyond. I am convinced that all the theological resources we shall ever need are already to be found in the people who, day by day, try their own particular kind of keeping faith.

You will quickly see the limitations of what I have written. I am simply trying to connect up a few of the threads of a hugely important conversation that is going on across many boundaries as we move into a new century. Our ability and willingness to share in that conversation and reach conclusions in which all feel they can share, conclusions which will continually need to be reviewed, will determine the geography in the Land of Unlikeness.

Nigel Collinson
August 1996

1. THE TWENTIETH CENTURY – ANOTHER LOOK

1.   A changed landscape

In 1840 William Turner of Oxford painted a watercolour entitled 'Portsmouth Harbour from Portsdown Hill'. When I saw the picture for the first time at the Royal Academy's exhibition of British watercolours in 1994 I instantly recognized it. The Isle of Wight can plainly be seen across the horizon, and to the right of the natural horseshoe of the harbour and in the foreground is Portchester Castle. A line of three-masted men-of-war ride at anchor in the harbour and beyond them, the merest smudges of darker colour indicate old Portsmouth and old Gosport. On the top of Portsdown Hill, three shepherds form a group with their dogs and sheep. The rest is empty landscape.

In a hundred-and-fifty years the landscape has filled up, changed almost beyond recognition. The bare bones of the scene are still there, the sea, the harbour, the Island forming the backcloth. But what has changed the scene for ever is people, hundreds of thousands of them and the densely packed houses of Portsea Island, Gosport and Fareham that go with them. The M27 now runs by the foot of the hill, past the impressive IBM complex. The new marina, Port Solent, is typical of this part of the world. When William Turner of Oxford painted his picture, the scene had changed little since the Romans found safe haven here. Now, as we move towards the close of the twentieth century, all is different.

And it is not just the outward landscape that has changed, with its vast urbanization. So has the internal geography, the mental landscape of the people who live there. For since 1840, along have come Charles Darwin and his unassuming rival Alfred Russel Wallace, Marx and Freud, Einstein and Picasso, Crick and Watson, quantum physics and the Hubble space telescope. The way we see ourselves and the way we see 'reality' have been changed utterly. The very presence of IBM, with its implied world of information technology, is a late-twentieth century statement in itself.

In January 1901, Cosmo Gordon Lang, Vicar of Portsea, stepped down to Clarence Pier in Portsmouth to meet the yacht, *Alberta*, bearing the body of Queen Victoria on its processional way from Osborne to London. He alone saw the new King, Edward VII, kneeling at the foot of the coffin and side by side with him the German Emperor. Lang, destined to become one of the

3

great princes of the church, thought it portended a new era of European harmony. How wrong he was! A dozen years later, the Great War marked the real beginning of the twentieth century.

When Lang ministered to St. Mary's Portsea, at the turn of the century, it was one of the most notable parish churches of the land. He had as many as sixteen curates and the vicarage opposite the church, now a funeral director's, was their home. One of them, Cyril Foster Garbett, was later to follow Lang as Archbishop of York. Lang's own bishop in Winchester (this was before Portsmouth became a separate diocese) was Randall Davidson. Lang followed him as Archbishop of Canterbury in 1930. Lang and his cricket team of curates ministered to the forty thousand souls of the Portsea Parish, preaching Sunday by Sunday to huge congregations. On his first Sunday in the parish, it is reported that Lang catechized over fifteen hundred children.

On the face of it, it seems that those who argue the decline of the church in the twentieth century have a lot of evidence on their side. There does seem to have been an immense falling away in British society from the institution of the church, and from faith itself. The facts seem to lie all around us and there are the memories of all those older churchgoers who recall a time when their church was full. On the other side of the balance sheet, however, is the historian, Kenneth Scott Latourette's record of the reported ignorance of the front line soldiers in the 1914-18 War of such basics of the Christian Faith as the Lord's Prayer. The Army Chaplains wrote home to their bishops in dismay at the situation. There is also an interesting recollection of Cardinal Heenan, in his autobiography, of leafy Ilford in the closing years of the last century:

> On Sundays we dressed uncomfortably. We did not play
> games, dig the garden or make a noise. That was the extent of
> the tribute our community paid to the Sabbath. My family
> and our Catholic neighbours, the Foleys, went to church at
> least twice a Sunday. Of the other hundred or so families,
> four regularly attended a place of worship.[1]

2. 'While we range with science'

What is undoubtedly true is that by the middle of the last century, as the new natural sciences began to show what they were capable of, and as huge movements of population from the countryside to the growing industrial towns took place, people's ties with their old religion were being loosened. Matthew Arnold, standing on Dover Beach in 1867, certainly seemed to think so. Listening to the sea's roar in the dark night, he heard only the 'melancholy, long, withdrawing roar' of faith. Charles Lyell, the geologist, and Charles Darwin, the naturalist, posed enormous problems for Christian thinkers. The time spans in which they, in particular, were teaching their contemporaries to think challenged the popular, more biblical ways of thinking. While creation was still thought to be only a few thousand years old, people could not only more easily understand Christian teaching, they could nurture their beliefs in God's special creation of humanity. Somehow, it was all on a more human, and, therefore, a more comprehensible scale.

But Darwin, catching something of the mystery of the rocks from his mentor, Lyell, began to think on an unimaginable time scale. How many aeons, he wondered, had it taken for the mighty Andes to be formed? What was 'the wonderful force which has upheaved these mountains?' he asked himself. On 20th February 1835, while the *Beagle* was visiting Valdivia in Chile, he glimpsed the answer, for he experienced an earthquake for himself, and to his astonishment discovered afterwards that its force had raised the beach on which he stood by a few feet. Fresh mussel beds were now *above* the high tide mark. Mountains might not after all have been created by one huge cataclysmic event but as a result of a series, immensely long, of smaller events.[2] What was required for that to happen was time, endless supplies of it. And that was precisely the requirement for the tiny changes in living species brought about by natural selection. The strait-jacket of biblical orthodoxy was abandoned. Few scientific people could contemplate holding on to it for a moment longer than necessary.

Darwin's thinking made its way into the culture of the times surprisingly quickly. Perhaps it caught the mood of Victorian optimism born of the miracle of progress that industry and its machines were bringing. Some voices, however, were decidedly cautious. Tennyson[3], in 'Locksley Hall Sixty Years After' (1886) wrote:

Is it well that while we range with Science, glorying in the Time,
City children soak and blacken soul and sense in city slime?

There among the glooming alleys Progress halts on palsied feet,
Crime and hunger cast our maidens by the thousand on the street.

There the Master scrimps his haggard sempstress of her daily bread,
There a single sordid attic holds the living and the dead.
(ll. 217-22)

There were, perhaps surprisingly, some clergymen who were prepared to meet the challenge of the new thinking. One was a country parson called Charles Kingsley. He was a leading member of the Christian Socialist Movement that was just coming into being as a result of just those sentiments that Tennyson expressed. He was also a brave man and far ahead of his contemporary clerics in his curiosity for the modern world. From Eversley, his parish in Hampshire, he wrote to Darwin in 1859 following the publication of *The Origin of Species*, full of praise for the book and this much encouraged Darwin himself. Kingsley also began to correspond with T. H. Huxley, Darwin's main protagonist. Huxley said of him that he 'was a very real, manly, right minded parson but I am inclined to think on the whole that it is more my intention to convert him than his to convert me. He is an excellent Darwinian to begin with . . .'4

Gradually, other Christian thinkers began to assemble their arguments, as well as to assimilate the new science of the late nineteenth century and the early twentieth century. It was after all taking place within a framework of thought which had been laid down almost three centuries before by Descartes and Newton. It was they who had, so to speak, made the rules of debate – experience, observation, measurement, hypothesis, analysis, rigorous thinking, reasoned debate and conclusions which could be tested. Christian theologians now used, as far as they were able, those same techniques in defence of the Faith. By the middle decade of the twentieth century the Christian Church seemed at least to be holding its own. It had held off the challenge of the logical positivists in the Thirties, people like A. J. Ayer, who for a time had taught that only what could be measured or somehow experienced by the senses counted as evidence. Anything else, said Ayer, was just non-sense.

3.   'Into the melting'

It was the publication of John Robinson's *Honest To God* in 1963 that alerted the British church to the fact that all was not well. The then Bishop of Woolwich dedicated his book to 'Stephen and Catherine *and their generation*'. It is interesting now to re-read his Preface:

6

... I suspect that we stand on the brink of a period in which it is going to become increasingly difficult to know what the true defence of Christian truth requires. There are always those (and doubtless rightly they will be in the majority) who see the best, and indeed the only, defence of doctrine to lie in the firm reiteration, in fresh and intelligent contemporary language, of the 'faith once delivered to the saints' . . .

At the same time, I believe we are being called, over the years ahead, to far more than a restating of traditional orthodoxy in modern terms. Indeed, if our defence of the Faith is limited to this, we shall find in all likelihood that we have lost out to all but a tiny religious remnant. A much more radical recasting, I would judge, is demanded, in the process of which the most fundamental categories of our theology – of God, of the supernatural, and of religion itself – must go into the melting.[5]

At the time, an older generation of Christian scholars assured us that it had all been said before. But many *of our generation*, raised on the traditional faith of our postwar churches and chapels, but increasingly restive with it for all its worthiness, had never heard the like. The thinking of John Robinson and his mentors, Dietrich Bonhoeffer and Paul Tillich, reshaped our Christian minds, sending us on a faith journey of restless exploration. Robinson's very chapter headings became our theological agenda – God was 'the ground of our being'; Jesus was extolled as 'the man for others' and responsible living took on the mantle of 'worldly holiness' guided by the 'new morality'.

Robinson's concern essentially was pastoral – how to communicate the faith to Stephen and Catherine and their generation. His insight was to understand that the old categories were fast losing their meaning, particularly the idea of a God 'out there', who stands outside time and space but who acts, some would say interferes, within both. 'Such a supreme Person in heaven is the great enemy of man's coming of age,' he wrote.[6] And in this latter phrase particularly – *coming of age* – he caught the spirit of the Sixties.

As he says in his Preface, John Robinson knew that the Sixties generation could not be won back by a stronger, clearer, more up-to-date presentation of the Christian faith of old. He had glimpsed the reality that somehow, as the twentieth century wore on, the world and how it understood itself, was changing. Science, if one can talk in such simplistic terms, had altered the way one could conceive of God's relationship to the world. Morality based on the traditional authority of the church and the State had apparently not served us well, judging by two world wars and the recurrent problems, which the Sixties generation was just discovering for itself, of mass starvation in what were known as 'the under-developed countries' and growing nuclear armaments in East and West.

So, against those who looked simply for a revival of religion, Robinson proposed, after Bonhoeffer, a 'religionless Christianity' and a church . . .

> organized not to defend the interests of religion against the inroads of the state (legitimate and necessary as this may be) but to equip Christians, by the quality and power of its community life, to enter with their 'secret discipline' into all the exhilarating, and dangerous secular strivings of our day, there to follow and to find the workings of God.[7]

His vision was a brave one, a necessary one, though by its very nature incomplete. Living so close to the momentous changes of the twentieth century, he saw, only a small fragment of what was happening. But he saw what he saw and he pointed to a way of keeping faith that enabled men and women of their own time to come to a realization of the presence of God without sacrificing their integrity.

John Robinson was looking not for a God who was out there, a-pathetic in the old sense of the word in that nothing could touch or change him, but for a God who was immersed in the most profound human experiences and longings, at the depth of our beings. Only such a God would keep pace with what at the time was perceived to be the march of secularism. I remember our college visitor gathering us students together in late 1963 and asking us how we felt about the training we were receiving and whether or not we thought it would fit us for the Methodist Church of the next ten years. 'What church?' I replied rather hastily. 'None of us think the church will be here in ten years' time!' This was the time for religionless Christianity.

For a while, it looked as if we were right. The late Sixties, on some accounts, emptied the college chapels in the universities; ministers and priests left the church in numbers to become social workers and teachers and the 'death of God' theology set in. But we were wrong, of course. Christianity survived our dire prophecies and theology took a turn towards the real instead. The experience of the poor in South America began to work new thoughts about

8

God's presence with his world; so did that of black people and of women. In short, other voices began to be heard, voices that came from the margins, voices to which the old power blocs had mostly refused a hearing until now. It was almost as if a terrible mid-century war, in which forty million people world-wide had been killed, had drawn something of a line under old theological thinking which had concentrated overmuch on the golden casket of truth handed on from one generation to another waiting only to be unpacked. Now another body of evidence was coming forward for examination, one that we knew only too well, for it was the world of our own experience as human beings. Theology could be incarnational in precisely that way. The Word could become flesh.

At about the same time, in a different but not unrelated context, the polymath scientist and philosopher, Michael Polanyi, reminded the readers of his seminal *Personal Knowledge* that in all human activity which seeks to discover knowledge, there is a 'personal coefficient'; what we are and our perspective on things actually plays a part in what we come to know.[8] It was, I think, John Robinson's personal coefficient that made *Honest to God* such a powerful and effective book for the Sixties generation. Here was not cool, academic, detached theology aimed at a timeless audience but a passionate and soul-searching account of the faith that was in him for the benefit of his children and their generation. It worked because it was personal, because it tried to take its context seriously and because it was above all direct and honest with its readers. Once theology steps out of the purely academic arena, important though that is, the personal coefficient assumes great importance. Theology is then seeking to appeal to its generation, to convince its audience, to defend the Christian position in thoughts and words that people will receive with understanding. It has entered into the realm of apologetics, a term that may be misunderstood because it sounds rather shamefaced. Nothing could be further from the truth in fact, because Christian apologetic is concerned with taking the challenges to faith without evasion. It seeks to understand the context of our lives, interpreting faith to those who may have very little understanding of traditional belief or who may be antagonistic towards it. But just as important is the care that we take with interpreting our context to the mind of faith and with being aware of our surroundings. Speaking about God might just have its roots in an appreciation of the achievements of human beings who follow other pathways of creativity.

At some point then, Christianity must attempt to speak to the culture of the day, to the context, but also crucially to listen to it as well. Of course, we are

9

all a part of that cultural context. We cannot help it. Indeed, we probably inhabit many interlocking worlds of culture at the same time. Culture is a difficult word to grapple with, but I like the definition given by Richard Niebuhr in his book, *Christ and Culture*. He called culture 'our artificial, secondary environment' which we impose upon the natural environment. Niebuhr says that it consists of language, habits, ideas, beliefs, customs, social organizations, inherited artifacts, technical processes and values.[9]

4.   Theology for the Third Millennium

The questions I want to ask are these. What is the particular cultural context in which we are thinking about God now, and what are the special characteristics of the very late twentieth century which compel our attention and which affect our belief in God? And what, in turn, has Christianity to contribute to contemporary debates and challenges within a world that finds itself at the centre of almost continuous change? The immediate stimulus for this question is Hans Küng's positioning of himself on the opening page of his *Theology for the Third Millennium*. He declares:

> We are looking for a new direction, we are developing a programme for a theology that is nowadays, more than ever, exposed to the manifold tensions, changing currents and divergent systems, and finds itself, as far as its grand tradition goes, in a crisis of credibility and plausibility; but that can make its way out of this crisis neither through an unenlightened, backward orientation to traditional forms of belief nor through glibly opportunistic strategies of adaptation to stylistic change in science and scholarship: and that can win for itself a new credibility and social relevance only through an intellectually responsible account of Christian faith which meets the demands both of the Gospel and of facing the third millennium.[10]

Küng is asking that, faced with the enormous challenges of the late twentieth century, those who argue passionately for the Christian Faith should not retreat into the past or opt out of the hugely important discussions that are going on at the moment, so many of which have fundamental relevance to the Christian Faith. Engaging with the times will inevitably mean risk and exposure but only by joining the fray will Christianity be seen as having a claim to be both credible and appropriate. If we are inclined to doubt the significance of what Küng is asking for, we need to ponder the words of the actor, Simon Callow:

> Were the god of Love not well and truly dead, buried at the Somme, Katyn, and Dachau, Aids would surely have finished him off.[11]

That is a particularly twentieth century statement of unbelief, almost Nietzschean in its dismissive certainty.

It was Friedrich Nietzsche who strode the mountains above Silvaplana in Switzerland in the early 1880s, '6000 feet above man and time', who declared that 'God was dead'. Writing of those he called 'the Afterworldsmen', which in German is very much like 'backwoodsmen', he declares:

> Thus I too once cast my deluded fancy beyond mankind, like all afterworldsmen. Beyond mankind in reality?
> Ah, brothers, this God which I created was human work and human madness, like all gods!
> He was human, and only a poor piece of man and Ego: this phantom came to me from my own fire and ashes, that is the truth! It did not come to me from the 'beyond'!
> What happened, my brothers? I, the sufferer, overcame myself, I carried my own ashes to the mountains, I made for myself a brighter flame. And behold! the phantom fled from me![12]

Is that what we have been doing for the last hundred years, carrying our own ashes to the mountain, frightening away God or even disposing of him, with our brighter flame? There are many who would say that is precisely what we have been doing and look where it has got us; a century which has witnessed greater suffering and barbarity than any in recorded history. Yet that is not the whole story by a long way. Some would argue, for example, that it is religion itself which has been at the heart of so much suffering, either as its direct cause or by advocating a God who is helpless to do anything about it. That is Simon Callow's point. And in any case, besides the misery of the twentieth century there is also the huge potential for human happiness and well-being. You only need recall the whole panoply of modern medicine. The fact is that the canvas is too big to make simplistic judgements.

But judgements are being made, and highly sophisticated ones too. In a recent article for *The Guardian* newspaper, the journalist, Linda Grant, wonders if the current *'fashion for religion'*, as she calls it, indicates a yearning for ethical values and meaning following 'the longest experiment with amoral materialism Britain has ever known'. Religion is a false guide if the twentieth century is anything to go by, she says, and she is, therefore, deeply suspicious of the religious faith of the leader of the Labour Party, Tony Blair. Her own recipe for the future is humanism:

> . . . when Christians ask me how I can bear the idea of a world that is not suffused with the love of Jesus and the hope of everlasting life, I want to say between gritted teeth, 'Oh, grow up.' To believe . . . in man, is to build a world out of what we've got.
>
> Two thousand years after the birth of Christ we are no longer drifting in a supernatural fog but have moved away from such explanations for the universe. The removal of God has not diminished it; rather, the huge shadow his presence casts over understanding no longer blocks out its true immensity and wonder. Do we really want, to lead us into the next millennium, a man who believes that the world was created by a deity who takes a personal interest in whether he breaks down over Lent and sips a quick whisky? To build a world based on human ethics and human values, rather than materialism and religion, is the coming task.[13]

The sharpness of her tone should act as a reminder of what the real argument is all about. Our keeping faith with God is not an idle theological debate about how many angels can dance on the point of a needle. It is about whether or not we have the nerve, the ability, the credibility, to contribute to the argument that is now raging about the values and goals that will shape things for the twenty-first century. What is at stake is not belief alone, what we believe and whether or not we can demonstrate that we are not 'drifting in a supernatural fog'. The issue is about the guides, the influences, the principles that will undergird us as we move into a new world, as Linda Grant plainly indicates.

The point is nicely illustrated by two of Charles Handy's recent books. Always in the vanguard of understanding the competing forces that affect our world, particularly in the field of economics and work, Charles Handy has changed his mind. In 1990 his book, *The Age of Unreason*, outlined his view of the way in which things were going in the world of work – flexibility, upside down thinking, rapid change, flat systems of management instead of pyramids of power within organizations. His view at the time was fairly optimistic. All of this would produce great benefits for everybody in a global economy. Four years later, in *The Empty Raincoat* he says that, although things have gone much as he predicted, he is not comforted by the thought because too many people have been affected adversely:

> What is happening in our mature societies is much more fundamental, confusing and distressing than I had expected . . . Part of the confusion stems from our pursuit of efficiency and economic growth, in the conviction that these are the necessary ingredients of progress. In the pursuit of these goals we can be tempted to forget that it is we, we individual men and women, who should be the measure of all things, not made to measure for something else. It is easy to lose ourselves in efficiency, to treat that efficiency as an end in itself and not a means to an end.[14]

That is a brave and far-sighted thing to say. It raises questions about the values which underpin our decisions and about the resources that sustain us. It alerts us to the fact that efficiency can be raised, and has been raised, to the status of a god and that much else that has to do with our being human can be forgotten. A faith which will serve us well in a new century will need to be a faith that not only nurtures our inner being, but one which can also sustain us at the edges, at the intersection of faith and living. To this end, it will be one that listens as well as speaks, learns as well as teaches, because we will need to understand how much the world has changed from the one in which Cosmo Gordon Lang stepped down to Portsmouth's Clarence Pier in 1901. I wonder if there is much now that Lang would have recognized?

2. END OF CENTURY

Just outside Yeovil there is the little village of East Coker. It is the archetypal English village with the most beautiful setting for its parish church. You approach it through an iron gate and up a long curving path. To the right of the church is the big house and to the left a lovely view over the fields. I call in most times I am passing, just to be quiet in the half light with the lamp above the altar burning steadily. If when you lift the latch of the church door you turn to the right, you will find what really draws me there. On the west wall is a plaque commemorating the last resting place of Thomas Stearns Eliot, 1888-1965. His family traced their roots back to Andrew Eliot who married Grace Woodier and emigrated to America from East Coker about 1660. So, before he died, Eliot arranged for his ashes to be brought back to the church at East Coker. On the wall plaque are inscribed not only his name but also the first and last lines from one of his greatest poems:

> In my beginning is my end . . .
> In my end is my beginning.
>
> East Coker.[1]

You might interpret those few words to mean that nothing changes but how wrong you would be:

> In my beginning is my end. In succession
> Houses rise and fall, crumble, are extended,
> Are removed, destroyed, restored, or in their place
> Is an open field, or a factory, or a by-pass.
> Old stones to new building, old timber to new fires.

All is ceaseless activity through the centuries, Eliot says, which gives point to his assertion late in the poem that 'Old men ought to be explorers'.

On my last visit to East Coker, I discovered another memorial tablet, this time to William Dampier, born there in 1651, who left the village to circumnavigate the world – which he did three times, on one occasion bringing back the original Robinson Crusoe, Alexander Selkirk – and whose journals Nelson gave to his midshipmen to study. What a curious irony – a native of East Coker in the depths of Somerset, who left to travel the globe, whose last resting place is unknown; and an American-born poet, the descendant of another traveller, born on another continent but with an unerring instinct for home.

This chapter is written in the belief that all our knowledge about God, and our relationship with him, is not only the product of much exploration, but *is* exploration. To explore the context within which we live is a way into the mystery of God just as certainly as is the life of prayer and contemplation. Indeed, they are two sides of the same coin and, just as we are altered in our travelling, so our faith is shaped by every journey of exploration.

The chapter is also written as a form of collage. Sometimes described as sticking bits and pieces together, collage belongs very much to the twentieth century. It was used by the avant-garde, chaotic Dada group of artists who flourished during the Great War and who were the precursors of the surrealist movement, and it has survived as a popular art form through to the end of the century. A verbal collage seems rather unlikely, but I will try to use it because, the idea of a verbal collage actually begins to describe where we are at this particular point. The more or less coherent world views of previous generations are breaking up – one only has to think of the old East-West divide – and no single 'big picture' has yet taken their place, nor on some readings of the situation ought we expect it to. Nevertheless we have inherited so much that is important for our own self-understanding and the picture now is changing almost as fast as it is being made. A collage is perhaps the most suitable way of describing the context in which we find ourselves.

Amongst the closing words of his *Into the Twenty-First Century*, having just sketched out the agenda for a church on the verge of a new era, Donald English says:

> What the Christians of Europe have to face is a mission field that is even harder to penetrate than was the world in the 19th century. The challenge is to allow ourselves to perceive what actually is happening in the world around us, what are the powers and groups who drive our society and its development, how the gospel of Jesus Christ addresses and is addressed by those sources of power, and how we may communicate the Gospel in the areas where they operate. There is no room for laziness, or sloppy thinking; for cosiness and self-protection in the church; or for asking God to do what we are not willing to make ourselves available to do. It requires a total review of

the life of the church in the light of the context, a reshaping which makes us available to those who need us, and a renewal of all our training programmes in the light of that task.[2]

It is that context that I am trying to describe in this chapter. The task is such a large one that I can do no more than point here and there. By and large I do not wish to express any value judgements now other than that, for me, this or that particular aspect of the picture is too important to be left out. That is why I am writing them up as a verbal collage. I am trying to display them without necessarily following them to their logical conclusion or exploring all the inner connections and contradictions. I am trying simply to display aspects of our cultural context, a context far too complex, too diverse, to have a single explanation. You will no doubt wish other things to be said. They can perhaps be the subjects of future conversations.

There is, however, at least one major pitfall in describing things in the way I am intending, 'at arm's length', as some would see it. It does rather give the impression that all of it is nothing to do with us, that we can simply stand back and view our world dispassionately. Whereas the opposite is the case. Human beings are very much involved both in shaping the world by our activity and in 'thinking' the world into being. That might seem a rather strange idea that we 'think' the world into being. Nevertheless, our language, our mental pictures, the inner connections we are prepared to make, all give form and substance to the world in which we live. In other words, we do not only live within the context, we are a part of the context. It shapes us, just as surely as we shape it.

One other thing has to be borne in mind and, from the point of view of our keeping faith, it is of first importance. Not only do we need to see ourselves as part of this verbal collage, but we need also to see it all as part of God's creative energy. It is a fundamental mistake to discuss God's creation as if it were all concentrated in the first moments, the biblical 'in the beginning' or science's 'big bang'. For when we talk about the creation of God, we are surely speaking about a process running through every aspect of the universe's life to which God is intimately related, and which does not stop. In that sense, the twentieth century in all its glory and shame reveals the creative and redemptive energy of God, which human beings can frustrate and squander but which they can also fulfil and enjoy.

The first requirement for a collage is a suitable background against which everything else can be displayed. For me that background is *the way things work*.

1. The way things work

Depending upon who you read or how you see things, you might come to the conclusion that what actually makes the world go round is variously clockwork, atoms, genes, tiny packets of energy called quanta, bits (binary units), the market or progress. These are invoked as the key 'mechanisms' by which our universe lives and moves and has its being. I want to hint at just two or three possibilities.

A visit to an old working mill quickly gives one the impression of how fascinating and useful the principles of the machine were to those industrialists of earlier times who harnessed the power of rivers or steam. Through a series of belts, levers, pulleys and wheels, energy is distributed to a hundred-and-one labour and money saving devices. It is not hard to imagine that the order of the machine could become a symbol for the way in which all well-ordered societies should proceed. The machine's powerful inevitability could even begin to encourage the belief that progress was inevitable. That was the way things happened! Cool, detached logic began to shape the thinking of the centuries that the universe itself could actually be understood in an ordered way and the perfect 'mechanical' symbol for this universe became the piece of clockwork. And it was more than a symbol. The ordered revolution of the spheres in their heavenly places was a description of how things were and a constant source of wonder. So Joseph Addison (1672-1719) could write:

> What though in solemn silence all
> Move round this dark terrestrial ball;
>> What though no real voice nor sound
>> Amid their radiant orbs be found:
> In reason's ear they all rejoice,
> And utter forth a glorious voice,
>> For ever singing as they shine:
>> 'The hand that made us is divine![3]

There is no doubting the success of the machine as a way of seeing how things work. It is reflected in our view of what an ordered society is. Many of us like things to go like clockwork with everything in its place. Others say it has

17

dehumanized people and turned them into cogs in an impersonal world, where job losses result from what is euphemistically called down-sizing; some say that it has devalued the natural world and made it into the equivalent of a huge gas station out of which human beings are content to pump its riches, or into a convenient waste bin into which they can dump technology's rubbish.

Small wonder that other views of how things are have made their appearance. Danah Zohar in her books, applying the ideas of quantum physics to what she regards as a more holistic understanding of the self and society, is bitterly critical of Newton's legacy:

> The immutable laws of history portrayed by Marx, Darwin's blind evolutionary struggle and the tempestuous forces of Freud's dark psyche all, to some extent, owe their inspiration to Newtonian physical theory. All, together with the architecture of Le Corbusier and the whole vast array of technological paraphernalia that touches every aspect of our daily lives, have so penetrated our consciousness that each and every one of us sees himself reflected in the mirror of Newtonian physics. We are steeped in what Bertrand Russell called the 'unyielding despair' to which it has given rise.[4]

For Zohar, the truth lies not in the solid, predictable world of Newton as she sees it, but in the realm of individual packets of energy called quanta and the ability of the tiniest electron to be either a particle, that is a single entity of matter in a particular place, or a wave of energy spreading its presence across a number of particular places. Indeed, it can be both wave and particle at the same time. The world of quantum physics is bewildering to those who like their feet on firm ground. Indeed, I am reminded of Dr Johnson who, discussing Bishop Berkeley's theory that reality depended upon someone perceiving it, kicked a stone in the gutter and exclaimed, 'I refute him thus!' I am also comforted in the face of a fascinating and beguiling subject, by the words of John Polkinghorne in his most recent book, *Serious Talk*, which returns time and again to quantum mechanics:

> Quantum theory in its modern form came into being during 1925-26. It was invented in order to describe the behavior of atoms, and it has proved consistently successful in all its applications since then. We use it now to think about the behavior of quarks and gluons, systems that are at least a hundred million times smaller than atoms. That is a very

impressive record of achievement. But the paradox is this; that though we can use it, though we know how to do the sums, and though the sums always seem to give the right answers, we do not understand the theory. We do not know what is going on. That is very odd . . .[5]

Bruce Mazlish, Professor of History at the Massachusetts Institute of Technology, returns to the subject of machines, not as a way of picturing how things work, but as the partners of human beings. His book, *The Fourth Discontinuity*, is about the 'co-evolution of humans and machines'.[6] Drawing on the surprisingly long history of the machine and the early belief, illustrated by Leonardo's anatomical drawings, that seemed to make the body into a machine of sorts, he concludes that human beings and machines of the most sophisticated kind are now part of the same evolutionary process, enjoying a mutuality that would never have been dreamed of only a few decades ago. What he calls *the fourth discontinuity* has been removed. Humans and machines are no longer entirely separate. Witness, he says, the reliance of medical science upon hi-tech of all kinds. The recent transplant of a mechanical heart into a patient too old for a human heart transplant seems to support his case; as does that strange phenomenon known as 'road rage', in which the car seems to function as an extension of the personal space we regard as inviolable and 'ours'. The notion that human beings and machines share a common destiny is explored increasingly in contemporary cinema, in unlikely but popular films like *Robocop,* for example. The ethicist, David Thomasma, writing from a somewhat traditional point of view and distrustful of our reliance on technology, says, 'In a megamachine society, we have the death of the human, the death of compassion, and a world wired for death.'[7]

Of course, there is also the computer. Nicholas Negroponte, Director of the Media Laboratory at the Massachusetts Institute of Technology, tells us that the 'change from atoms to bits is irrevocable and unstoppable'. What is a 'bit'?

> A bit has no color, size, or weight, and it can travel at the speed of light. It is the smallest atomic element in the DNA of information. It is a state of being on or off, true or false, up or down, in or out, black or white. Bits have always been the underlying particle of digital computing, but over the past twenty years we have greatly expanded our binary vocabulary to include much more than just numbers. We have been able

to digitalize more and more types of information, like audio and video . . .[8]

So Negroponte begins to verbalize the digital core of what he and others believe will be the Third Wave (Alvin Toffler's phrase), following the agricultural and industrial revolutions, where interface agents will act for us, smoothing our path through a global network of ever more sophisticated computers in which 'the haves and the have-nots are now the young and old'. Some, like Douglas Hague, are suspicious of titles such as ' information super-highway' or 'the information revolution'. However, he is in no doubt that it will be the young in our schools, with the right teaching, who 'will push their way into a further revolution, one for which, as yet, we have no name'.[9]

Once there was only one feasible explanation of how things work. That explanation was God. He was the guarantor of all things, the prime mover, the first cause. Now there are many explanations of how things work and the intriguing thing is that each one might be valid depending on which level you are on, from which perspective you are viewing things. However, just because we are offered more than one rational explanation for how things work does not mean that we can dismiss them all out of hand and descend into anti-intellectualism and go for explanations which are superstitious and unintelligent. We still do, of course, but such a faith will draw us away from the world of the twenty-first century and make us seem increasingly quaint to the point of absurdity.

The background for the collage then, is the different views of how things work. They represent the basics of our understanding. Against that back-ground, rather grandly, I want to apply our changing ideas of time and space.

2. Time and space

Time and space are not what they were. When Dampier left East Coker to travel the world, he was provided with a plan of where 'things' were by late-renaissance map-makers using the latest advances in the understanding of perspective, so that he had a bird's-eye view of the world.[10] There was much map making still to be done, but Dampier would have known the relative positions of the continents. The spaces between them, marked by the oceans, were measured in the weeks, months and sometimes years that were taken to cross them, given favourable weather. Space and time were fixed quantities.

The growing realization of our century has been that space is being annihilated through time. Here is Negroponte again:

> In the same ways that hypertext removes the limitations of the printed page, the post-information age will remove the limitations of geography. Digital living will include less and less dependence upon being in a specific place at a specific time, and the transmission of place itself will start to become possible.[11]

We see the effects of this in the way in which the financial economy of the world is now instantly global. I am told that, at the beginning of their day, workers on the Indian sub-continent, educated in English and computer-literate, receive 'down the line' work that has been done by their counterparts in London, work on it themselves and return it in the same way so that their London colleagues can continue it at nine the following morning. The earth's time zones are heaven-sent for those whose horizons are big enough. In a global economy, space is annihilated through time.

Is the traditional idea of a God who is timeless and eternal attractive to those, especially a younger generation, who live within such time horizons? It might be, if those same people find all this unnerving and long for some kind of sheltering stability. On the other hand, if they are exhilarated by watching a tidal wave of capital surging across the globe, as the hero of Tom Wolfe's *Bonfire of the Vanities* is before his downfall, then they would find such a God irrelevant and profoundly boring. At very least we would need to call up an old idea, the one that talks about a thousand years in God's sight being as yesterday when it is past and as a watch in the night (Psalm 90).

So the verbal collage now consists of a background of ideas about the way things work, across which we have begun to hang some revised ideas about time and space; but then, in time and in particular places, certain historical processes begin to take shape. Amongst these is how we organize that most basic of human activities, our work.

3. How we organize ourselves

The earthquake that struck the southern Japanese city of Kobe and the surrounding area on 15th January 1995 caused dreadful damage to the city and its inhabitants. A friend from Japan recently wrote to me about the scale of the damage – six thousand people killed, thirty thousand injured, over a hundred thousand homes and buildings destroyed. It also had an unforeseen effect on the way in which one of the world's great car companies organizes itself; it dislocated part of the production of Toyota cars. In the 1950s, Toyota pioneered a philosophy of lean production called 'just-in-time' which eliminated the need for huge stocks of materials, tying up capital and human resources. Described by Francis Fukuyama as 'an extremely taut and fragile manufacturing system that can easily be disrupted by problems anywhere along the line from supply to final assembly',[12] its demands are team-work and the ability of each worker to see the whole rather than the part. Its benefits are improved quality and, presumably, worker participation and responsibility.

How different from the old style of motor car manufacture and supply, Fordism, as the economists call it, after its American inventor Henry Ford. Fordism required huge numbers of workers operating in continuous shifts, living close to the plant, which was in itself a huge machine with the production line at its heart. It tied up vast quantities of raw materials at one end of the process and resulted in equally large stocks of the finished product at the other. Our railways prospered as a result but often vast amounts of capital were, in effect, to be seen in railway sidings waiting for delivery. The just-in-time philosophy is aimed at putting an end to this.

Incidentally, before we move too far away from Henry Ford, we should note how, for good or ill, the changing ways of making and selling motor cars seem to act as some kind of a bell-wether in the fast-moving world of business management. *The Economist* reported recently on 'Ford 2000', Ford's strategy to create a global business by integrating its American and European businesses, with the aptly-named Ford Mondeo leading the way.[13] Globalization is an unavoidable concept in the late twentieth century. Whether or not it can be achieved and then sustained seems to be the subject of much debate.

Hamish McRae describes some of the results of lean production techniques:

> In many fields the optimum size of a factory is diminishing; economies of scale are coming to matter less than nearness (both physically and culturally) to the market; electronic management of production, where goods are tailored to meet demand signalled by data transmitted from cash registers in retail outlets, means that it is more important to have a factory which is nimble in switching product lines than one which can churn out identical items at the lowest cost. Italy's highly successful fashion knitwear retailer, Benetton, by making up all its garments in grey and dying to order, is able, using up-to-the-minute sales data, to re-stock its shops with the most popular colours in a matter of days.[14]

In the same way, an American jeans manufacturer will measure you in the shop, digitally transfer your particular size and design requirements to the factory and provide you with a pair of jeans that are made-to-measure. Moreover, they will come complete with your own personal barcode stitched in so that next time you will not even need to be measured. It is known as mass customization, which seems a contradiction in terms.

In a just-in-time world, human resources are hired to offer particular skills, often through an agency, on short-term contracts. Pay and conditions are fixed locally not nationally. The emphasis is on training, re-skilling and flexibility. Computerization and electronic communication seem to have revolutionized the banking industry where, in the growing field of telephone banking, people are trained in three weeks in the use of an on-screen script from which to work through the customer's inquiries. Previously it would have taken five years' training and experience to get to the same point. The world of work becomes increasingly individualized and, for some people, increasingly lonely. The downside of a just-in-time world is that workers might once again come to be seen as hands. The good side is that people do have jobs when work is increasingly in short supply.

You might well ask what are the implications of all this for faith and our understanding of God and the role of the church. It seems to be a world apart from theology. That is a mistake we have made before; indeed, we have been making it for the past two hundred years, ever since the beginning of the so-called industrial revolution. The churches caught up with urbanization and industrialization too late. The result was that in the last century the church buildings tended to be in the wrong place, denominational competition set in so that in the end there were too many buildings as Robin Gill[15] has reminded us. The gospel that was preached was rural rather than urban, remote rather than accessible. By and large then, the church's ministry, with some honourable exceptions, was seen as unsympathetic to the new and often cruel circumstances in which people lived and earned their daily bread. Small wonder that the industrialized population of the western world lost contact with the Christian Church. There is a whole sad literature about it.

For example, there is Walter Rauschenbusch, the founder of the social gospel movement in the United States, who in 1907, published his *Christianity and the Social Crisis*. Greatly influenced by Sydney and Beatrice Webb during a year's stay in Europe, partly in Germany and partly in the Webbs' home in England, he came to realize, from first-hand experience as a pastor of the Second German Baptist Church in New York, that the social and working conditions of the crowded city in the 1890s were inhospitable to traditional morality and religion:

> It would be a theme for the psychological analysis of a great novelist to describe the slow degradation of the soul when a poor man becomes a pauper. During the great industrial crisis in the 90s I saw good men go into disreputable lines of employment and respectable widows consent to live with men who would support them and their children. One could hear human virtue cracking and crumbling all around.[16]

Now, almost a century later, we are moving into what some are calling a post-industrial age, at least in the West, and it is important to try to understand the uncertain world in which people are trying to make a living. Charles Handy describes an increasing part of that context as a portfolio world, in which men and women work for a variety of employers at the same time or offer a range of tailored skills:

> Professionals, the knowledge-workers of all types, are obvious candidates for portfolio lives. So are those who make things, the traditional fixers and makers like plumbers, builders, carpenters, and electricians, but now, also, the new fixers: the agents, brokers, conference-organizers, house-finders and sitters, travel agents and tour-arrangers. These are the new servant businesses, often one or two partners with a suppor-

ting cast of occasional stringers; the cooks, drivers, gardeners, health specialists, language-teachers, child- and house- and dog- minders, cleaners, even, I am told, people you can pay to change your light bulbs. Here are also, the old crafts: the potters, weavers, bakers, painters, writers, computer software-designers and photographers.

Read the Yellow Pages in any city, anywhere, to find the portfolio world. These people charge for their produce not their time.[17]

Forty years ago, one of the great pioneers of industrial mission, Bishop Ted Wickham, studied the churches of industrial Sheffield and his pioneering words still have a haunting ring. He reminded us of the church in history, 'called as she is to "baptize" the common life of *man*, and to become incarnate within successive cultures, and point them to God and their own true destiny'.[18]

4.   The way we are now

The fourth, and for our purpose, the final application to this verbal collage is a series of indicators of our values, our character, our goals. They overlap, derive vitality from one another, have varying shapes and colours, are not all that could be said. They certainly are not finished products, issues now ended and viewed objectively. Quite the contrary; we see them only partially because, for good or ill, they still have enormous vitality. In a sense they represent aspects of our spirituality.

1.   Elaine Showalter has written about the recurrent motif of uncertainty about sexuality at the close of centuries. All the anxieties with which we are familiar, of changing roles between the sexes, of uncertain morality, of sexual identity itself, were all to be found in the closing years of the nineteenth century. They actually seem to belong, she says, to the atmosphere of fin de siècle. The final sentence of her book, *Sexual Anarchy*, suggests several possible outcomes: 'What seems today like the apocalyptic warnings of a frightening sexual anarchy may be really the birth throes of a new sexual equality.'[19] One thing can be said with certainty. It is difficult to exaggerate the importance of the recovering of women's history or of the perspective and persistent energy of women. It is also extremely difficult to write about without seeming patronizing, an oddly appropriate word in this context if ever

there was one. The extent to which women have been rendered invisible by the way in which history has been written or literature has been studied is becoming more understood. In the narrow lens of biblical studies, Elisabeth Schüssler Fiorenza has pointed out the irony of St. Mark's story of the Passion in which the betrayer, Judas, and the denier, Peter, are remembered by name, but the woman who washed Christ's feet and of whom he said that her act of kindness would always be told in memory of her, in fact has no name.[20] More broadly, Virginia Woolf wrote in 1929:

> Towards the end of the eighteenth century a change came about which, if I were re-writing history, I should describe more fully and think of greater importance than the Crusades or the Wars of the Roses. The middle-class woman began to write.[21]

When Emma Thompson received her Oscar for the screenplay of Jane Austen's *Sense and Sensibility*, she underscored the importance of that change. *Sense and Sensibility* was published in 1811; it still comes as a surprise to recall that only five years later, Mary Shelley was writing *Frankenstein*. Both women, Jane Austen and Mary Shelley, have found the twentieth century's own art-form, that of the moving image, particularly hospitable. Increasingly women are at home in film, not only as players but as directors and producers – amongst others, Jane Campion (*The Piano*) and Diane Keaton (*While You Were Sleeping*).

2.   The world of the cinema is one hundred years old this year. Probably human beings have always created images, but the movie camera could only be the product of a society already sophisticated in science and its applied technology. In other words, the cinema belongs specifically to the modern age in a way that few other art forms do because it combines the creativity of the two cultures, the arts and the sciences, which we seem to keep apart in most other places. Those who have no sympathy for the big screen will regard it purely as a marginal form of entertainment. On the other hand, those of us who from almost our earliest days have been captivated by all that films can do for the imagination and our own self-understanding will perhaps respond to the words of the American film director Martin Scorsese who, in a recent television personal view of cinema's one hundred years, having confided that once he thought he was destined for the priesthood but then discovered that his vocation was to make films, offered his view that perhaps cinemas and

churches were very much alike. They fulfil the spiritual need that people have to share a common memory, he said.

3.   One of the abiding images of the twentieth century is a photograph of the whole earth, blue and green and flecked with white cloud. It was provided by one of the moonshots that the United States made in the 1960s, unbelievably now thirty years ago. For the first time human beings saw their home in its entirety. What had been guessed, calculated, explored by the old sailing ships, romanced about in literature was seen to be the case. There is only one earth. Coming at the end of the Sixties, it gave an enormous boost to an ecological concern that had been stirred with the publication of Rachel Carson's book, *The Silent Spring* (1962), which alerted us to the effects of pesticides upon the natural world. The Green Movement expressed a growing unease that the science, technology and commerce which had promised to feed the world and produce ever-expanding living standards for all, did so at the expense of a spreading degradation of the planet. Moreover, it produced wealth for the few and left the many untouched, except that their burden of poverty and debt was increased. We sensed the growing problem in the wasting of our western cities.

4.   The stark reality of poverty is a recurrent nightmare of our century and one of our greatest causes for shame. In one sense, all the cost of our technology to Mother Earth might be justified, although some would argue vociferously with that, if we could now say that the poor of the world, by whatever standard they are judged to be poor, are feeding themselves, being housed, educated and employed. Regrettably, there has been a fearful asymmetry about it all, a terrible lack of justice, and by and large we have not cared enough. Some now worry that, far from improving the lot of the world's poor, late twentieth century technology, will in fact, make things worse. We are told that Tokyo has more telephone lines than the whole of Africa. It does not take much thought to see where the money will continue to go, thereby magnifying the asymmetries. We are beginning to see the rise of modern city states built on islands of new technology; they will increasingly be isolated from their poorer neighbours. At the most basic level, one of our most precious resources will be water. Hamish McRae says that the rising world population will increase the problem: 'Water needs to be treated as precious immediately, for shortages will become grave in some parts of the world within one generation.'[22]

I can do no more than hint at the huge canvas on which we are living in this, our own fin de siècle. There are some who feel it has more than a whiff of decadence about it, of a way of life which is running out of steam, going badly wrong. Equally, there are those who are tremendously excited by what they see, who welcome the breaking down of old certainties, who treat technology as an ally rather than as a Frankenstein monster and who celebrate difference and diversity. However we view it, the context of our lives will affect our beliefs, our values, our ultimate perspective and they, in turn, will shape a new century. This is not to say that for the future, Christianity can be reduced to questions of lifestyle, although lifestyle is an issue for more and more people and might, just might, turn out to be a crucial way of keeping faith for the twenty-first century. There has been no century, I think, more able to reflect upon itself, in which human beings, many of them at least, have been able to step outside their own small lives and see their world more or less as a whole. Television and newspapers enable people who are increasingly well educated to do that. We are no longer as likely to be controlled by the guilt or ignorance that religion has encouraged in the past. As the actor, Tony Robinson, recently remarked in answer to why he had not had his children christened, 'I felt the idea that children wouldn't go to heaven if they weren't christened was barbarous. If God was like that, I'd rather go to hell.'[23] Ironically, as I will try to show in the next chapter, our generation has not always been successful in finding something to put in religion's place and too often has fallen victim to old superstitions, new authoritarianism or a despairing nihilism that says that in the end nothing much matters any more.

3. FUTURE CHOICES

1. The End of History . . .?

There are different analyses of where we are at the present moment, some optimistic, some pessimistic. Towards the optimistic end of the scale is that of Francis Fukuyama and his suggestion that we are at 'the end of history'. Written in the aftermath of the fall of the communist bloc, Fukuyama says that we are at the end of history in the sense that there is now no large battle left to fight which might create significant history. History is directional and it is moving, and in fact has already moved decisively, in the direction of liberal democracy. It is liberal democracy which has been shown to outlast its greatest opponent hitherto, communism. Thus we are at the end of history. Fukuyama's view is essentially optimistic. There is such a thing as progress, he declares, but his optimism is threatened by only one thing, boredom. In his closing pages he gives a warning glance over his shoulder:

> If men of the future become bored with peace and prosperity, and seek new thymotic struggles and challenges, the consequences threaten to be even more horrendous (than the great wars of this century). For now we have nuclear and other weapons of mass destruction, which will allow millions to be killed instantly and anonymously.
>
> Standing as a bulwark against the revival of history and the return of the last man is the imposing Mechanism of modern natural science . . . the mechanism driven by unlimited desire and guided by reason.[1]

Fukuyama's description of modern natural science as a 'mechanism', coupled with his appeal to reason, places him firmly within that Enlightenment tradition which many are now calling into question. Increasingly common is the opinion that the world view which took its origins in the seventeenth century, what is often called the Enlightenment project, and which has shaped our world, is now beginning to falter and is, in fact, in crisis. The traditional understanding of the Enlightenment was that it was a way of looking at the world and our place within it that was based on reason. This appeal to rationality took its cue from the work of Isaac Newton and René Descartes in the seventeenth century and led more or less directly to the rise of modern scientific investigation and the industrialization of the western world. It is that world view that many are now saying is faltering under the weight of problems

29

which are of its own creating – pollution, consumerism, the terrible wars of this century, continuing mass starvation, the ambiguity of science and technology, apathy, trivialization and disillusionment. Those who argue this way would dispute the whole idea of progress which underlies Francis Fukuyama's concept of directional history. There is no evidence, they say, that demonstrates beyond doubt that the twentieth century is moving towards the goal set by the Enlightenment. On the contrary, it has been the most destructive century on record, with the environment increasingly degraded and more human beings killed by the deliberate act of others than in any previous one.

One result of this dissatisfaction with or even repulsion from the modern world is irrationality. Reason has failed to deliver all that it promised, therefore, we will abandon reason. To a degree this accounts for some of the wilder claims of religion. If reason cannot be trusted absolutely, belief in the supernatural, the occult or the frankly absurd does not sound so bad. In fact, to people desperately seeking 'something', it might even sound attractive. The rejection of reason, however, often leads to the elevation of narrow views, based on sect or race or country, to the status of dogma which cannot be challenged. It is much easier to demonize your opponents if you have abandoned or lessened your appeal to what is reasonable. It was, I suspect, for this reason that the French philosopher, Michel Foucault, was so guarded on the subject:

> If philosophy has a function within critical thought, it is
> precisely to accept this sort of spiral, this sort of revolving
> door of rationality that refers us to its necessity, to its
> indispensability, and at the same time to its intrinsic dangers.[2]

Yet even those who are most committed to the rational approach are beginning to see that in practical terms it does have its problems. Ernest Gellner is uncompromising in his allegiance; he calls it 'the one genuinely valid style of knowledge'.[3] It offers a view of the world which is sound, no matter in what part of the world and in which cultural setting we live. It has produced, through science and technology, enormous benefits for all those able to share them – but Gellner admits that those benefits are not distributed evenly across the world. That is not rationalism's only shortcoming. For the individual in a crisis, it is 'too thin and ethereal' to be of sustenance and, in any case, it is too abstract for most people. In other words, for all its ability to give an accurate picture of what the world is like and to achieve real progress, the path of reason is not sufficient and most people will need more. This reminds me of nothing so much as the remark of the dying Alex Jardine, former Bishop of Starbridge in Susan Howatch's *Ultimate Prizes*, to the modernist Dean, Neville Aysgarth: 'I discovered that the Modernist road leads eventually into a void. If you pursue certain radical approaches far enough you end up with nothing . . .'4

That is the ultimate fear of those who now suggest that the Enlightenment project is in crisis. Not only has it not fulfilled the human dream, the sceptics say, it has produced a death-dealing technology which is leading to the denial of human values. 'The world is not working', says Jim Wallis plainly on the opening page of his *The Soul of Politics*.5 What are the alternatives?

2. The Postmodern Turn

One currently fashionable alternative is postmodernism. Notoriously difficult to define, everything that can be said about it will be contradicted because it is more a mood, an attitude than a well-defined movement, and there are many forms of postmodernism. On the one hand, postmodernism takes modernity for granted; cars, planes, telecommunications and information technology, two world wars, nuclear physics, modern medicine, cinema, the growth and decay and revitalization of cities – all that I tried to describe in the previous chapter goes without saying. That is what might be called postmodernity. There can be no returning to a world behind or before them except on nostalgia trips. The curious thing is that nostalgia is now very popular, almost as if people would like to shake off the effects of modernity. There is thus one form of postmodernism which Hal Foster calls 'a postmodernism of reaction'6 which is about recovering the traditional. One sees it in the reaction to 'modern' architecture, for example.

In other places, notably in the study of literature and language, philosophy, the social sciences and theology, the turn to the postmodern is more 'suspicious' of the way things are and tends to want to peel away all the skins, the facades, to seek out the underlying and almost forgotten shapers of attitudes and beliefs. There is, as it were, a piece of archaeology to be done. This is the postmodernism of resistance, of reading against the grain, of deconstruction. Often such a process reveals the way in which one group exercises power and domination over another group, with belief structures coming into being which support the dominant power. One of Foucault's major pieces of work was in

31

the area of what he called *panopticism*, a method of exercising control and power over great numbers of people in society. He borrowed the idea from Jeremy Bentham, the eighteenth century British philosopher, who suggested the panopticon as a way of enabling one person to supervise large numbers of inmates – it consisted of a courtyard of buildings divided into cells with a central observation tower. Foucault uses that notion as a way of describing the intricate ways in which the powerful exercise their hold upon society.

Foucault wrote: 'The "Enlightenment", which discovered the liberties, also invented the disciplines.'[7] There lies, I think, the heart of the postmodernism of resistance; not the rejection of modernity but the fundamental questioning of Enlightenment ideas which have given birth to the modern world, a suspicion of detached observation, of the cold application of rationality, of the belief in progress and utopia, of universal theories which impose their own tyranny on what otherwise would be a world of difference and diversity. There is no grand narrative, no foundational theory that explains everything, no blueprint and no transcendence. To the discomfort of those who like things to be cut and dried, boundaries become indistinct. Is Foucault's work history, sociology, philosophy? Postmodernism reflects the world of the late twentieth century; increasingly, the boundaries which represented order and a settled way of understanding things are breaking down.

Clearly, postmodernism issues a profound challenge to our keeping faith, but as Clive Marsh has said:

> Postmodernism sharpens up the questions which any defender of Christian faith has to address truly to be defending faith today (rather than talking in a vacuum, or as if the audience were from the last decade or the last century) . . .
> The basic challenge to Christianity – and it is a serious one – is whether Christianity itself must join forces with postmodernism, not for the sake of its own survival (it could easily survive regardless of whether it is true), but because it appears to be the only path to tread with full integrity.[8]

Consider the resonances that are set up when you place side-by-side, resistance and protest-ant; situated-ness and incarnational; the text and the word; the suspicion of powerfulness and the recovery of those voices from the margins to which Christianity is increasingly listening. What we are continually looking for is a way of conversing with postmodernism so distrustful of old dogmatic certainties. That is why, in the next chapter, I want to explore a little further the idea of conversation and modest faithfulness.

Here is Sallie McFague, doing postmodern theology by way of metaphor, using the idea of mother, lover and friend as models of God:

> For our time the new models are illuminating, helpful and appropriate ways in which to think about the relationship between God and the world. And that is all that is being advanced, in as much as metaphorical, heuristic theology says much but means little. It is mostly fiction, mainly fleshing out a few basic metaphors in as deep and comprehensive fashion as possible to see what their implications might be. Perhaps the imaginative picture that has been painted provides a habitable house in which to live for a while, with doors open and windows ajar, and with the promise that additions and renovations are desired and needed.[9]

Is postmodernism a real alternative to the Enlightenment processes of the last two or three centuries which have provided, no matter how unevenly, a basis for the development and government of the western world at least? Or is it, as its critics suggest, just a passing fad that belongs especially to the well-cushioned world of a comparatively few academics and intellectuals? What of the relativism to which it tends, the understanding that one interpretation is as good as another? Does this not lead to a belief that in the end nothing matters very much? If so it is hardly a basis for a programme which will keep the world on track and put bread into people's mouths.

Despite the criticisms, postmodernism represents a set of question marks against all the traditional, cut and dried answers with which we too easily buttress our lives. David Harvey identifies four 'shifts' within our century, which, he says, are especially important to note. Examples of each of them can be found in the previous chapter:

1. Difference and 'otherness' are key factors in understanding social change. He specifically includes race, gender and religion.

2. 'The production of images and of discourse' – film, television, literature – they create a symbolic order within which we all live.

3. So, too, do the changing dimensions of time and space.

4. Our understandings are not closed and fixed; they are open-ended and capable of being discussed.[10]

Perhaps, after all, we have been a little too confident, believing that we in our powerful, reasonable and mainly white, male, western world had the measure of everything. Postmodernism acts as a counterpoint to all that. However, postmodernism as such does not of itself offer a comprehensive, alternative worldview. It is too fragmented and, in any case, it would surely go against the grain to impose itself. The postmodern mood does, however, open up the agenda and that is important. Patricia Waugh puts it like this: 'I suspect that Postmodernism will increasingly come to be seen as a strategy for exposing oppressive contradictions in modernity.'[11]

3. The 'Me' Generation

Curiously, one end of the postmodern spectrum fuses with late twentieth century capitalism to produce a very powerful form of individualism which has been popularly called the 'me' generation. One of the buzz words on the lips of politicians and economic managers at the moment is 'flexibility'. We are told that a country's economic success, on which hang personal security and social stability, will depend upon the flexibility of its workforce. Thus for the best part of two decades we have seen the dismantling of old professional and vocational attitudes and of trade union power in favour of personal decision and local bargaining. Old groupings have been atomized because they have been felt to hold back progress. Long established communities which had gathered around a region's traditional industry have been scattered as their products became unfashionable or too expensive. Ironically, the communications revolution has hastened the process. When it is that easy to communicate, not everybody has to be in the room or even in the same country.

A recent consultation of senior Human Resource Managers and Counsellors at St. George's House, Windsor, took as its theme, 'People and the New World of Work'. Its report noted:

> If the trend towards individual measurement, individual performance, career resilience etc. develops, it is likely to cause a mismatch. Some counsellors warn that a star

performer in an extreme arena of 'everyman for himself' would look alarmingly like a psychopath. Even in milder versions, the strain of short-service contracts, working alone or in short-lived teams, not belonging anywhere and owing allegiance only to him/herself calls for considerable emotional robustness and internal strength. How many could cope with such a life, or even want to, must be a question.[12]

What starts out as desirable – flexibility – combines with insecurity to produce the 'me' generation. What matters is my agenda, my future, my family, my rights. We adopt a rugged individualism in which old codes of morality and ways of doing things based on group attitudes are given up in favour of what pleases me. Now, without doubt, you have to place alongside that what Charles Handy calls 'the Bob Geldof effect', the way in which through the brilliant production of images (see Harvey above!) people can be moved to 'Feed the World'. Nevertheless, in what lies behind the 'me' generation we have a very powerful, often negative, motivating force in our lives and one which has to be reckoned with. It is interesting, therefore, to see another buzz word beginning to be used – community – and its active ingredient, 'communitarianism'.

The columnist, Julie Burchill, recently pondered the question of what kind of religion fills the gap in the lives of the 'me' generation left by the retreat from the Judaeo-Christian ethos. Her view is that superstition fits snugly:

> In the past . . . I would primly maintain that superstition was okay, while religion was wicked because there had never been any major wars between those who refused to walk under ladders and those who touched wood. From a less self-righteous but more actually righteous perspective, it is also blindingly obvious that while Christianity leads people to commit acts of random kindness upon their fellow man, superstition – and its meretricious kissing-cousin mysticism - begins and ends with the worship of self.[13]

4.   Fundamentalism

Fundamentalism is alive and well. It ought not to be, according to some postmodernists who tell us that such ideological thinking is dead. The fact remains that religious fundamentalism is a growingly powerful, political force and provides a coherent, although many would say a doubtful, platform for getting things done. It has followers in great numbers who are prepared actually to back their beliefs with action. That constitutes its undoubted strength.

At one level, much of Christian religious fundamentalism is a reaction against modernity, seen most clearly in the creationist views it has of the origins of the universe – the biblical stories of creation got it right; and in its rejection of much contemporary sexual morality – it is strong on the family and, by and large, against abortion. On the other hand, the fundamentalists have embraced some aspects of modernity with a gusto that has been lacking in their more liberal colleagues. It is the Christian Right who have been the most enthusiastic users of the media and it is they who make full use of information technology in the interests of evangelism.

I think it is probably true, although at first sight it seems unlikely, that Christian fundamentalism may be viewed as a distant cousin of Enlightenment thinking. After all, the Age of Reason led men and women to believe that the world was orderly enough for it to be explored and for objective truth about it to be gathered. In a similar way, Christians believe the world to be orderly because God created it to be that way and, therefore, truth about the world and God can also be known, but this time by revelation and by the study of God's word.   Put differently, 'Rationalism was the continuation of exclusive monotheism by other means', said Ernest Gellner.[14] In both cases, scientific humanism and Christian fundamentalism, objective knowledge is highly prized. Knowledge about the world or about God does not depend upon your perspective, who you are and where you happen to be standing. It exists outside you. It is real. That is why in fundamentalist churches there is so much emphasis upon *teaching*. Faith needs to be backed up by as much sound knowledge about God as the believer can take in. It is this knowledge which creates the world view which will sustain and nourish the believer in life.

We might also think that fundamentalism is a response of a particular kind to change. This might account for its growing strength at the end of this century, particularly as this end-of-century has a millennial ring about it. It is now twenty-five years since Alvin Toffler alerted us to what he called future shock. His main thesis, and he was writing from a general not a religious viewpoint, was that the future was even then breaking into the present at such a rate that human beings had difficulty in coping. They were 'future shocked'. Some developed stability zones, places of safety where they could be themselves and which enabled them to deal with change. Those stability zones might be major things like a home or a relationship. Equally, they could be as mundane as a car, a particular habit or even an old suit. Toffler says that if we are to manage the huge changes that are overtaking us, some of which I tried to indicate in the previous chapter, we will need to develop very powerful tools, 'patterns of relative constancy in the overwhelming flux'.[15]

Viewed from this perspective, fundamentalism becomes a potent response to the uncertainty and change in which we all find ourselves. It can, of course, be empowering, enabling human beings to find their one fixed point. It can also diminish people, preventing them from growing and discovering their full powers. All religious responses have those two possibilities within them. If we are tempted to brand other people's thinking as fundamentalist in contrast to our own, the remark of Terry Eagleton in his *Ideology* ought to keep us humble:

> . . . one person's rigidity is, notoriously, another's open-mindedness. His thought is red-neck, yours is doctrinal, and mine is deliciously supple.[16]

5. Making choices

There are, then, at least three possibilities to be considered if the way of reason is now being called into question, three possibilities which offer alternatives for reflection and action – postmodernism, individualism or the 'me' generation, and fundamentalism. But is the way of reason, the legacy of the Enlightenment, really in the sort of crisis that forces us to choose in such a way? Stephen Toulmin reconfigures the problem. He comes to the conclusion in *Cosmopolis* that the rationality which for three centuries has shaped western Europe and given birth to science, technology, politics, nation-statehood and all the artistic expressions that go with them – Modernity – is being *humanized*. The world has been found not to be as stable and certain as a piece of clockwork; human beings have discovered that they are an integral part of the natural world. One after another, disciplines of thought and action which once might have been seen to be independent – medicine, nuclear physics, technology of many different kinds – are now re-adjusting their sights as we have begun to ask questions about quality of life and cost to the environment. Human beings have begun to modify their programme and their ways of solving problems because that is what the situation demands; the processes which began in Europe almost five hundred years ago have changed step, but they have not run out of steam. Toulmin writes:

> As we approach the third millennium, our needs are different, and the ways of meeting them must be correspondingly rethought. Now, our concern can no longer be to guarantee the stability and uniformity of Science or the State alone: instead it must be to provide the elbow-room we need in order to protect diversity and adaptability.[17]

Toulmin's insistence that Modernity is being humanized takes us right back to his understanding of the origins of the Enlightenment project itself. The usual picture of those beginnings is that, in what was thought to be the stable, increasingly prosperous first half of the seventeenth century, with the power of the church over people's lives on the wane, the thinking of Descartes and the mathematics of Newton provided the ideal platform for the rise of natural science grounded on calm reason and observation. In fact, says Toulmin, a proper reading of the period reveals great instability, with Protestants and Catholics at each other's throats and the great French hope for peace, Henri IV, assassinated on 14 May 1610. When his heart was brought back to be enshrined in the Jesuit College at La Flèche, north of the Loire, which he had founded in 1603, who should be in the congregation to see it all but a young student called René Descartes. For most of Descartes' life, the Thirty Years' War raged in Europe, a war both of politics and religion when religious truth was a central and divisive issue. Within such a divided Europe, the certainty of Descartes and the confidence of Newton had great attraction for those who came increasingly to distrust theological dogma and the uncertainty of princes. What came to be forgotten was the late renaissance humanism of the previous century, Leonardo, Shakespeare, Erasmus, Rabelais and Montaigne. They, too, were reasonable people. At a time when the new explorers were opening up the four corners of the earth and bringing back their treasures and their adventure stories, they, too, were learning to celebrate diversity and difference. Neither did their humanism mean that they were hostile to religion. On the contrary, 'by their own conscientious lights', says Toulmin, they mostly saw themselves as sincerely religious and advocated a broad, humane openness. It is not difficult to see how such a tolerant humanism could be swept aside in the following turbulent century as people looked for certainty.[18]

So Toulmin argues that Modernity, as we have come to know it, had two roots, both equally rational. For two centuries, the rationality of Descartes prevailed. It looked for certainty by returning to first principles and starting to build an edifice, be it a scientific theory, a method of government or an industrial base, from scratch. Only in this last century has the cold logic of this kind of rationality begun to be humanized once more as we have seen how human beings are interconnected with one another and a part of the ecological whole. No longer do we imagine that the slate of human experience can be wiped clean:

> There is no way of cutting ourselves free of our conceptual inheritance; all we are required to do is use our experience critically and discriminatingly, refining and improving our inherited ideas, and determining more exactly the limits to their scope.[19]

6. A critical, contemporary Christianity

Whether this humanized Modernity is best described as simply the third phase of Modernity or as something so radically new that it has to be called Postmodernity is a matter of judgement. However it is named, Toulmin's central point is that what is needed now is for 'us to reappropriate values from Renaissance humanism that were lost in the heyday of Modernity'.[20] All of which leads me to wish to make a case for what I will call *a critical, contemporary Christianity* as a practical way of discerning the times we are in and fashioning our response; critical in the sense that we make 'discriminating use' of all the knowledge and ideas that are available to us; contemporary because, although we are deeply rooted in the Christian tradition, our interest, concern and sympathy are yet in the diverse world of human experience and creativity.

What would be the marks of a critical, contemporary Christianity and of a church that sought to embody it? Broadly speaking, there are five features. Taken together, I believe they represent a way of keeping faith for times of great change.

39

1.   A commitment to the interpretation of the Christian understanding of God, rooted in a biblical tradition which is shared by at least two of the world's major faith communities. At its heart is the creative presence and redeeming love of God which for Christian people is focused in Jesus Christ.[21]

2.   A decision to measure the tradition of faith against the demands of the present day in all their concreteness and challenge. It is in the intersection of the eternal gospel with the particular and changing circumstances of our lives that we will discover for ourselves what it means to keep faith, both in our believing and in our living.

3.   Its manner is one of excitement and humility; excitement in the sheer breadth and complexity of human knowledge and creativity; humility because all of us see in a glass darkly but, in Hans Küng's words, we are 'open to learn and ready to discuss'.[22]

4.   Critical, contemporary Christianity is truly ecumenical. If that word carries the full weight of its meaning, 'the whole created order', it expresses a move away from parochialism and individualism, from an over-concern for labels and practices which exclude, towards a determination to set the gospel against the widest horizons.

5.   Such a keeping faith which is rooted in God's loving purposes for humanity is people-centred. This means that:

–   human beings cannot be reduced simply to a collection of genetic or any other kind of information. Being human has a value which transcends the sum of its parts.

–   we have the means of discovering that which makes for our peace and healing.

–   we have within us a deep-laid sense of obligation to others which can be expressed in active citizenship. My guess is that the notion of the city, with all its long history of human coming together and mutual responsibility, will increasingly force itself to the forefront of our thinking because it is there, perhaps because of, rather than in spite of our 'green' convictions, that we shall express what it really means to be human.

40

Hamish McRae hazards the opinion that 'the glue holding a city together will increasingly become cultural and social, rather than economic'. This is because information technology will move people away from the centre of cities. Cities which have developed 'a high intellectual and cultural base will prosper at the expense of those which have not'.[23] Some four hundred years ago, the great cities of Europe were home to Erasmus, Shakespeare and Leonardo. Now, a new European spirit is in process of creation, in which the cities of Europe will enjoy a new prominence alongside and linked technologically with the burgeoning cities of East Asia, of the Gulf, of North and South America. A critical, contemporary Christianity will have its part to play in shaping attitudes and witnessing to the enduring longing of the human spirit to seek after God.

This does not at all ignore the reality of many of our cities now. In the 1995 Reith Lectures, the architect, Richard Rogers, gave a grim reminder of the catastrophe that awaits if we continue to let our cities decay. He was still optimistic, however:

> My cause for optimism in the face of grim evidence comes from the growing acceptance of ecological thought worldwide. Scientists, philosophers, economists, architects, and artists, often working with local communities, are now using a global perspective to explore strategies to sustain our future.[24]

Alongside Richard Roger's guarded optimism for the future of the city, we need also to hear the more general warning of the closing paragraphs of Eric Hobsbawm's history of the twentieth century, *The Age of Extremes*. In many ways it seems a personal history. He recalls, for example, the 30th January 1933 not as just another day in history when Hitler became Chancellor of Germany, but as 'a winter afternoon in Berlin when a fifteen-year-old and his younger sister were on the way home from their neighbouring schools in Wilmersdorf to Halensee and, somewhere on the way, saw a headline. I can see it still, as in a dream'.[25] So will we not take him seriously when he reaches the conclusion that 'behind the opaque cloud of our ignorance and the uncertainty of detailed outcomes, the historical forces that shaped our century are continuing to operate'.[26]

Many questions remain to be answered, about the wisdom to use technology wisely, about our ability to hold on to human values, about the moral strength of our institutions and our continued belief in their future. A critical, contemporary Christianity represents a viable approach to these issues. It transcends the selfish individualism of the 'me' culture; it suggests a meaning to human life that is denied to the fragmentary world of postmodernism; it offers the possibility of receiving others' gifts which is fundamentalism's greatest shortcoming. Finally, it takes seriously the extraordinary diversity of what it means to be human, both for good and for ill, within the economy of God's creative and redeeming purpose.

4. CONVERSATION

1. A network of conversations

There are many kinds of conversation. Some are what are called 'exchanges' and can refer either to a casual trading of points of view or to a heated argument. Then there are 'briefings' which can last for ages and consist mostly in imparting information. There are discussions, interviews, debates, chats and gossips, all of which consist of two or more voices making points, questioning and answering, confiding, hectoring, cajoling, pleading and threatening. There are even 'audiences' where being seen is as important as being heard and 'hearings' where it is important to know how to speak, and when. There is also that lively conversation between colleagues in which the desire is to formulate policy or come to a decision where the issues are not clear and, in the cut and thrust, a new and hitherto unsuspected possibility emerges. Even between rivals who see no chance of agreeing, a conversation in the presence of a mediator, with each one prepared at least to listen, may allow an unexpected alternative to present itself. There are also those times which often begin after a meal with friends and which go on long into the night, when old memories are rekindled, ancient trust invoked and the conversation develops a life of its own. Conversation really is a very human affair.

Conversation is a particularly appropriate way of doing our thinking about God and faith at the end of the century because it carries with it the assumption that we are looking one another in the face as those who are equals, both in giving and receiving. We are playing down the dogmatism implied by saying, 'This is what you must believe.' That sort of attitude has a very top-down feel about it and, if there is one thing we know about how people are increasingly feeling about themselves, it is that we do not respond well to being told. To some extent, the world is being re-made to bring it into line with people's sensitivities on this issue. You catch the change in the negative response to words like hierarchy, centralization and authority. We are beginning to feel uneasy with 'power' words, with ways of saying things that appear to put people under duress or at a disadvantage. Instead, we are learning the value of negotiation and consultation.

It is presumably to reflect something of this, that people like Charles Handy are telling us that increasingly organizations will become 'flat', with the pyramids of power being stripped out, leaving men and women to work together in teams, using their freedom creatively and responsibly.[1] If that is to happen, lots of conversations will be required. The worldwide web of the Internet will facilitate many of those conversations. They will skip over boundaries of nationality, time zone, gender, culture or censorship, although already there are warnings that the technology, which could put everybody in touch, will, in the end, lead to even greater isolation, with the poor and the old, the technological 'have-nots' excluded, while the communicating is being done by a comparatively small number of the technologically rich leading safe and comfortable lives. To that scenario we must return later. In the meantime, the 'network' becomes a very powerful symbol of the way human beings relate to one another; indeed, it is becoming more than just a symbol, more a working model of how things get done. Essentially, networking is a cluster of relationships built around a whole range of conversations.

There is a practical application to all this; we see it in our willingness to weave together the experience and opinions of different people in the room. I first became aware of it, although I did not fully understand its importance, in a series of workshops almost twenty years ago led by the Methodist minister, Dr George Lovell. At the time, he and a colleague were pioneering a way of working with groups of people which he called community development. He was in the process then of setting up a service agency for the churches under the name of AVEC, French for 'with'. His method of working 'with' people in groups was always to respect what people said about the issue under discussion so that instead of arguing against a person's point of view – because we often have our own agenda which we want to impose – we immediately and without question wrote it up, on a board or a piece of paper, and displayed it for all to see. That enables a number of things to happen.

Firstly, more people contribute, even the very shy, because they are not afraid of losing the argument or of looking silly. Secondly, the point becomes common property; it is not just that person's point of view; she or he is much less defensive about it and is willing to see it added to or altered in some way. People have even been known to forego their idea completely, knowing that it has been dealt with seriously in this way! Thirdly, as more and more opinions are brought to light for all to see, there is the possibility of discerning how all might move forward together. In effect, what is being facilitated is a conversation which recognizes that there is more than one way of being right. Many voices are required for an acceptable course of action to emerge and what makes it right is the willingness of those voices to accommodate each other. Along the way there will be surprises if we will allow them and negotiation takes time. We need to be patient. We will also discover that because we are different people woven together, truth will make itself known in unexpected ways. The notion of being woven together also protects the integrity of all the strands within the conversation. The strands remain strands, individual identities within a larger whole. That is important because each needs to know that her or his point of view is being taken seriously and that a sense of individuality is being respected. We are who we are, not just the raw material for other people's decisions.

It is in the light of these possibilities which 'conversation' allows, that I begin to view our thinking about God. The conversation may indeed be between two or more people or it could be the open and sometimes agonizing wrestling of the individual with a book or a thought or an experience. In the ensuing 'conversation' a new truth comes to light or, perhaps less certainly, we gain enough truth to help us on to the next conversation and so on. David Tracy has used this idea of conversation to understand what it means to interpret what he calls a 'classic' – it could be, for instance, a book, a belief or a film. Just as we give ourselves to a conversation, prepared to listen to someone else, prepared to be questioned, prepared to take risks, so we might give ourselves to the business of interpreting, for example, the Bible or a modern poet. After we have engaged in this 'conversation', interpreter and classic inter-acting with one another, it is just possible that truth will manifest itself. That is the interesting thing about some conversations. When we have been prepared to risk ourselves in real and open conversation, going with the flow of the words, acknowledging the silences, respecting the other's integrity, challenging one another with questions, quite suddenly the truth manifests itself. For an instant it seems to be located not in any of the partners to the conversation, but 'out there' in the open, almost visible. Tracy writes:

> Through that questioning we participate in the conversation of all humankind, living and dead. Through that conversation, we experience those truths made manifest by our willingness to dialogue and by the classics' power to disclose. That power manifests itself to every true conversation partner. Anyone who has experienced even one such moment – in watching a film, in listening to music, in looking at a painting, in participating in a religious ritual, in reading a classic text, in conversation with friends, or in finding oneself in love – knows that truth as manifestation is real. And it does suffice.

> Without such a truth, life is indeed nasty, brutish, and short.
> Without manifestation, thought is too thin.[2]

Mostly, this truth which manifests itself will only be what Tracy calls 'relatively adequate'. It is not the whole truth. We shall want to submit it to yet another conversation and more will emerge.

An analogy of this might be the computer and its program, Windows, with which I am typing this text. On the screen at the moment there are perhaps two hundred words. I can scroll them up or down to see more of the document – I'm revising it – and if I wish to, I can bring up another document and read it at the same time. I can transfer sentences or whole paragraphs between the two. For the moment the computer occupies my whole attention but I know that what I am seeing on the screen represents only a tiny fraction of the 'world' that is contained in it. Not only are there documents in there which I have long since forgotten and which will have to be cleared out one day, there are things that I know nothing about, programs far beyond my ability to use, unseen and, for me, unsuspected powers of arranging strings of 1s and 0s, just waiting for a certain key to be pressed. My computer has far more complexity, more potential, than I will ever fathom. For the moment I can read and change what is on the screen. I can type in more text, vaguely aware that I am not putting it directly on to the screen, although it appears there instantaneously, but rather making electrical connections deep within the computer's private world. For me it is something of a mystery, this interface between my mind and the computer. I see only a tiny fraction of the whole and I do not know how big that 'whole' is. What is onscreen is a 'window' into the uncomprehended. For the moment that window is relatively adequate.

2. A theology at ease with itself

I want to persevere with the idea of thinking about God and faith as a kind of conversation because it is a theology at ease with itself, a theology with the fear taken out of it, the fear of being excluded. A theology at ease with itself, one that is conversational in its approach to our understanding about God, offers us two things which may be of use to us now. It rejects exclusiveness and it also suggests a way of matching our tradition of faith with the realities of the world.

A theology at ease with itself is a theology that is not afraid to talk face to face. Once theology was done almost exclusively in the universities. I have on my study wall at home an old print, given us by friends in Oxford, depicting the scene in the Divinity School, one of Oxford's oldest institutions. Either side of the large hall is a pulpit, in which the two scholars stand debating their respective positions, answering questions, speaking, in Latin. Their learning was communicated orally and no doubt it was refined in the process. Today the universities and colleges are still proper places for that theological conversation; to judge by the popularity of theology courses, it is seen as a creative way to ask important questions. However, God questions have also come out of the universities precisely because they are people questions too. Because theology is about endings and beginnings, about citizenship and responsibility, about meanings and denials, it is an intensely human affair and belongs to the world of talk and earnest debate.

Speaking in Athens as he received the Onassis Prize in May 1993, Václav Havel, President of the Czech Republic, reminded his audience that politics had been removed from the very place where it had originally started, the agora or square of ancient Athens, 'a place where political decisions were reached through dialogue as citizens enjoying equal rights talked to one another directly, face to face'.[3] Sadly, said Havel, because life has become more complicated the politicians have been removed from everyday contact with the very people they are supposed to serve and the communication between them has to go through party structures and the media. In a similar way we constantly need to rediscover theological conversation; people arguing, debating, discussing face to face, what it is to keep faith. That will mean crossing the dividing lines that so often keep us apart, creating so much misunderstanding and fear. Especially is that true of the old fault line in churches local and national, the one that divides so-called liberals, radicals and evangelicals from one another.

When you turn to the biblical record, speech represents the time-honoured way in which human beings came to understand the presence of God in their lives. From the haunting question of God to Adam in the old creation myth, 'Where are you?', to the Word made flesh in John's Gospel, to the dialogue which Paul favoured in the synagogues of a dozen ancient cities or with the wise people of Athens, it is speech which either discloses the presence of God or hides it. The New Testament scholar, James Dunn, has shown how diverse and sharp were the conversations about keeping faith in that collection of writings, how many different and competing strands were woven into the fabric of the New Testament itself.[4]

Now I am asking for a particular kind of conversation, one which is not threatening or destructive, but one which is determined to hold on to such things as mutual respect, honesty and true sympathy. It is one that might enable us to see each other as human beings rather than theological adversaries and might even in the end lead us away from bigotry. Reflecting on the New Testament story (Mark 9:38-39) of the disciples trying to get Jesus to stop an unauthorized preacher and healer – 'Master, he's doing it in your name but he's not one of us!' – John Wesley declares a position of tolerance way ahead of the times even as we read him again in the late twentieth century:

> What if I were to see a Papist, an Arian, a Socinian, casting out devils? If I did, I could not forbid even him, without convicting myself of bigotry. Yea, if it could be supposed that I should see a Jew, a Deist, or a Turk, doing the same, were I to forbid him either directly or indirectly, I should be no better than a bigot still.[5]

His test seems to be: what contributes to genuine human well-being; are we helped to understand God or are we prevented from doing so? It is not that we are careless of error or absurdity or inadequacy, it is simply that we are also aware that we can never be absolutely sure, that there is more than one truth and that our best chance of real understanding is, together, to weave truth, being rigorous in our own thinking and generous to that of others.

3. In the Land of Unlikeness

Casting our thinking about God and faith in the form of conversation brings a crucial perspective into view, the perspective which I began to explore earlier, the land of unlikeness. Perhaps our situation is rather like a graph, the horizontal axis of which represents the fascinating variety of human experience as one century begins to make way for another, and the perpendicular axis our theological inheritance of faith. In the correlation, or 'conversation', between the two we would pinpoint the questions and responses for our keeping faith in the land of unlikeness. As it is, I have earlier attempted to describe our contemporary experience as a verbal collage which has four layers:

- our view of the way things work
- the changing dimensions of time and space
- how we organize ourselves
- the way we are now – our values, goals and character.

Those four, and others that space forbids me to include, represent an end-of-century perspective against which, as a conversation, we begin to interpret the tradition of faith that we have received. Hans Küng sets the conversation within an atmosphere of crisis both for theology and more importantly for the human community. Amongst the issues we must face seriously now, he says, are these:

- the end of 400 years of western assumed superiority – hegemony – and the development of other centres of power and influence;
- a profound ambiguity in science, technology and industrialization;
- social antagonism – exploitation, repression, racism and sexism;
- a distrust amounting to cynicism of the notion of progress;
- the encounter of Christianity with other religions 'on the basis of rough equality';
- historical catastrophes – Auschwitz, Hiroshima, the Gulag Archipelago, two world wars, continuing mass hunger;
- the suffering of women and those dependent on them.[6]

What Hans Küng and David Tracy propose is that we are now at a new stage in our thinking. Christian thinking has passed through stages that could be labelled successively, Jewish, Greek, Medieval, Reformation, Enlightenment and scientific, all of which influenced it, re-interpreting, giving it appropriateness to the times. We are now in another crucial phase of re-casting our theology, a new paradigm, in which the 'critical correlation' between the tradition and the particular concreteness of the times is vital. It is a kind of conversation, but one in which it is important to realize that the traffic is two-way; it is not simply a matter of identifying the contemporary questions and challenges and then finding the appropriate answers in the tradition. That is not a true conversation at all. It is simply one side trying to communicate by shouting louder. No, we must have the courage to perceive 'the always-already-not-yet event of Jesus Christ' who 'enters history ever anew to upset all calculations'.[7] There is one element in the conversation that could only happen at this particular moment, because it has taken the best part of the century to mature sufficiently; the conversation must happen ecumenically. Half a century ago, William Temple called the ecumenical movement 'the great new fact of our era'. Now, if we have the courage, we can begin to cash in the value of that.

In this ecumenical conversation between the tradition of faith and the demands of the contemporary situation, there will be those who will want to go for the fundamentals of the faith. They will recall us to those ways of being faithful which the past enshrines. I can understand that. For all of us, tradition can stiffen the nerve, enhance, encourage, pass on its treasures of wisdom. It can link us to the historical Jesus. That is tradition's greatest gift through writings, memory and history. On the other hand, tradition can also ossify into lofty superiority and indifference. It can elevate the past at the expense of present need.

That is why the correlation of tradition with the times is so important for a critical contemporary Christianity. It provides us with the framework for making decisions using all our faculties of mind and spirit. It affirms the importance of our heritage of faith and at the same time confirms one of the central tenets of the Jewish-Christian tradition, that this world must be taken seriously. It is also a recognition, in the complexity of the conversation which follows, of Walter Lippmann's saying, much quoted by the broadcaster Alistair Cooke, 'To every human problem, there is a solution that is simple, neat and wrong.'

4.   Relative Adequacy or Modest Faithfulness?

And on that note, we must return to what David Tracy called 'relative adequacy'. In any conversation, when truth manifests itself, Tracy says that it will do so with relative adequacy. For some that is a bitter pill to swallow and the need for certainty will take them in the direction of fundamentalism which brooks no doubt, no second opinion. On the other hand, if everything is relative, if no opinion is seen to be of greater worth than any other, then the charge that nothing matters very much at all must be taken seriously. The fact remains that between those two extremes, most of us manage to construct a matrix of values and knowledge out of which, by intuition and judgement, we must be able to decide what to do and to believe. We rarely stop to consider how we got there; for the most part it is second nature. It is part of our personal history, of how we came to be what we are. Sometimes, when our actions might hurt others or when the issue is particularly complex, like quality of life issues in medicine, we may stop and think. This just indicates that there is a tacit conversation going on within us and around us all the time unless we have become so detached from our own humanity and that of others, that another, grimmer, side of us has taken over. In fact, there lies the Achilles' Heel of all our human knowing. It is not the knowing that proves difficult, it is the doing, especially when the doing involves cost to us.

There are two reasons why I prefer 'modest faithfulness' to 'relative adequacy'. Both expressions underline the fact that we are not claiming too much. We recognize our limitations and the claims of other people upon us. Sometimes we will screw ourselves down to the sticking point and say, 'This is where I stand.' But mostly our understanding is more modest. 'Modest faithfulness' goes a little further, I think, and assumes our personal responsibility and involvement. Tracy uses 'adequate' to describe that truth which manifests itself out of conversation and it is important to recognize that it does not all depend upon us. However, 'adequacy' seems a little cold and has a 'take it or leave it' feel about it. If however, from our conversation, something appears to be the modestly faithful thing to do or to believe, we are recognizing our connection with the tradition that has brought us to this particular place and the cost of embracing it.

I think that ultimately it will be our readiness to acknowledge the modestly faithful nature of our decisions and our judgements that will be our salvation. It is a proper place to be. It will require us to listen sensitively to other voices, to be prepared to defer to others' points of view while explaining patiently our own. Sometimes it will involve being prepared to meet others half way in the knowledge that mostly our understanding is partial. In uniting our understanding with that of others we might even discover a greater truth. Will we have to give up our own truth, our own allegiances? Or are we being asked to mix everything up in some unacceptable search for the lowest common denominator? Not at all. What, through conversation, we are being called upon to consider is that two truths could actually exist and work in parallel with each other rather than in competition, almost over lapping, but drawing back from the conflict that nearly always arises when we have an immodest inner belief in our own certainties.

Writing about Erasmus, the great Dutch humanist who spanned the fifteenth and sixteenth centuries, a recent biographer, Léon-E. Halkin, says this:

> . . . our century as it draws to its close feels itself to be in agreement with him on several points: the awareness of a civilization in peril, a brotherly search for peace, the formation of a European spirit, a concern for rational education, classical culture, ecumenism, conciliar and postconciliar reforms, and finally Christian humanism and critical Christianity.[8]

One could wish that it were so, but one also recalls that Erasmus was followed by bitter divisions in Europe when the search for new certainties and the maintenance of old ones caused unknown suffering. Whether or not the new Europe will make us secure enough in ourselves to allow us to take the more humble route of relative adequacy or modest faithfulness remains to be seen. Those who comment on these issues are not confident. Hamish McRae talks of the possibility of a fundamentalist revolution in the west, not in the form of Christian fundamentalism but of 'secular populism', but with the same effect, the 'aggressive assertion by the majority of its values which are then imposed on the various minorities'.[9] Will Hutton, speaking about the future of Britain, says, 'The public realm must be reclaimed. Dialogue and inclusion must become political imperatives.'[10] Nor can we forget Eric Hobsbawm's description of xenophobia and identity politics as flourishing 'on the ruins of the old institutions and ideologies, much in the way weeds had colonized the bombed ruins of European cities after the Second World War bombs fell'.[11] If any of them is anywhere near the mark, genuine conversation may come to be seen as a highly desirable foundation for our common life and, yes, for all intuitions after God too.

5. ARE WE GETTING AHEAD OF GOD?

1.   Wonder and unbelief

In a recent Radio Four series, 'Devout Sceptics', the broadcaster Rosemary Harthill interviewed Dr Jonathan Miller about his attitude to faith. Jonathan Miller talked about his profound wonder at the glass of the cathedral at Chartres. Did not his sense of wonder lead him to God? No, came the reply. He was just as likely as any believer to have a sense of wonder but in this particular instance it was that human beings had come to such a place on the tree of evolution that they were capable of such magnificence. Perhaps it is not so strange that different people can look at the same evidence, Chartres Cathedral, and one marvel at the creativity of human beings, another at the source of that creativity's inspiration. After all, it is another example of the art of conversation, of there being more than one side of the argument. In this case, better to listen and learn.

Here is another contemporary expression of unbelief. It was found in a magazine called *GQ*; the author, Alan Jenkins, is talking about his attitude to marriage in church:

> More conventionally it's marriage that takes place in the sight of God, and the first hint most of us have that there might be more to marriage than a stag night, a p***-up and a honeymoon, then business as usual, comes in the vows themselves . . . 'to have and to hold . . . forsaking all other . . . as long as you both shall live'. Do we really have to buy this, when we no longer buy the God it's said to please? When we know so much more – and what we know is Darwin, evolution, all that – and biology tells us, whatever we do, our genes make us do it? . . . A bad patch, a build-up of boredom, a temporary defection or disaffection – would that be enough to drive me into someone else's arms, into adultery? I'd like to think not, I tell myself that I believe there's something sacred about my marriage, anyway. That's one of the reasons why it hasn't happened yet.[1]

I get the impression that the appeal to Darwin is not just a sophisticated excuse. The author belongs to an educated generation. Darwin does count. In this instance, 'Darwin' may be nothing more than shorthand for something that the author may not fully comprehend. Who can blame him for that? Darwin and his contemporary expositors represent the best explanation of how things have come to be as they are in the world of living things and I have no wish at all to argue with that, but where does Jenkins get his sense of 'sacred' from? Is the word used merely in a casual way or to fill a rather poetic blank space in much the same way that Stephen Hawking seems to talk about God? Or is there really somewhere within him a small protected space which influences his attitudes to what is right and wrong and confers 'specialness' and meaning on some things rather than others? If it is, it may be rather like the background murmur that the cosmologists assure us is all that remains of the Big Bang.

What we do know is that the old and often supernatural explanations no longer fit with the way people experience the world. It is often said that the scientific, technological culture of the twentieth century has pushed God out of people's lives, at least so far to the edges of their lives that he is no longer an option worth considering. Quite literally, there is no longer anywhere apparently that we can reasonably put him without embarrassment. God has been displaced from most people's worlds. At the same time, so this line of thinking goes, we are allowing ourselves to be cut off from the very things that make our humanity special – a feeling for the natural world and for human community. Small wonder that the world becomes a hostile place where we come to expect harm. Therefore, we insulate ourselves from it. We avoid eye contact and involvement. All of this has a profoundly alienating effect upon us. There is a loss of connectedness. We have been diminished.

But is this the only possibility? Is there no other way apart from the gradual slide into the lonely world of fearful individualism, the frightening end-game of the mechanical universe? At this point, please forgive what may seem a rather strange excursion. After I had written the next few paragraphs, I glanced back over them and decided to omit them or at least re-write them. As it is, I am inserting these few sentences, courtesy of my computer, because I have just been having another look at Richard Dawkins' *The Blind Watchmaker*, the sixth chapter headed 'Origins and Miracles' in particular. The result is that the man in green trousers and the porous world stay in. The more I read of Dawkins the more I come to respect him; more of him later.

2.   The man in green trousers

I saw him on the London train one morning going from Southampton to Waterloo. Had he been wearing the customary blue or grey suit, I would probably not have noticed him. It was those bright green trousers that singled him out and he was talking to two women. In the course of the conversation, the older woman mentioned that she had come up from Swanage that morning. The following Sunday, as luck would have it, I was to be in Swanage. At about 9.30 on the Sunday morning, I drove my car on to the car ferry for the short journey across the mouth of Poole Harbour, having just missed the previous ferry. When I drove off on the Swanage side who should be sitting at the wheel of the first car waiting to get on the ferry but the woman from Swanage who had been talking to the man in green trousers!

I make no claims at all for this complete coincidence except that I would probably not have noticed her but for the man in green trousers. The coincidence needed a trigger of recognition. It has since led me to think that perhaps the world is a little less cold and impersonal than we mostly suppose it to be. I would say that it is more open-textured than we think. If we have a sense of isolation, of alienation even, then perhaps it is a picture of the world that we ourselves have imposed upon it. I recognize that some people's experience of the world is so painful that a bleak outlook on things is entirely understandable. I want to hold on to the possibilities of coincidence, however. They represent a quantum of uncertainty, of unpredictability, in a world which we too easily dismiss as cold, neutral, deterministic.

Thomas Hardy's poem, 'Afterwards', is not about coincidence but it does talk about the importance of recognizing small pieces of connectedness and it has almost an aura of reverence about it:

When the Present has latched its postern behind my tremulous stay,
    And the May month flaps its glad green leaves like wings,
Delicate-filmed as new-spun silk, will the neighbours say,
    'He was a man who used to notice such things'?

If it be in the dusk when, like an eyelid's soundless blink,
    The dewfall-hawk comes crossing the shades to alight
Upon the wind-warped upland thorn, a gazer may think,
    'To him this must have been a familiar sight.'

If I pass during some nocturnal blackness, mothy and warm,
    When the hedgehog travels furtively over the lawn,
One may say, 'He strove that such innocent creatures should come
        to no harm,
    But he could do little for them; and now he is gone.'

If, when hearing that I have been stilled at last, they stand at the door,
    Watching the full-starred heavens that winter sees,
Will this thought rise on those who will meet my face no more,
    'He was one who had an eye for such mysteries'?

And will any say when my bell of quittance is heard in the gloom,
    And a crossing breeze cuts a pause in its outrollings,
Till they rise again, as they were a new bell's boom,
    'He hears it not now, but used to notice such things'?[2]

I find it interesting that Hardy wrote for a different generation, in a different setting from our own post-industrial age (as it is sometimes called) and yet even then, one who 'used to notice such things' deserved a poem. Connectedness is as much in the eye of the beholder as between things, people or events. Some people are able to see the connections, appreciate them, respond to them; whether those connections are miracles of engineering, of nature or of human relationships. Others are oblivious, now as in Hardy's day.

3.   Porous world

My colleague, Mervyn Willshaw [3], has been grappling with one of the deepest questions in all religious thinking; how we understand the providential presence of God in our world and in our lives, especially at times of suffering. God's presence is not in doubt, but it is on the mystery of how God draws the creation towards wholeness that Mervyn concentrates. He also asks the question, 'What place for prayer?' He ends like this: 'Through it all we may, in John Macquarrie's memorable phrase, help to make the world a little more "porous to the divine reality".'[4]

What if the world actually is porous? For the last two centuries or so, the world has seemed quite the opposite, hard and solid, machine-like, a piece of clockwork moving regularly with one thing leading inevitably to another. If things are so predictable, so unyielding, so densely packed together, why do unpredictable things happen? Accidents, coincidences, the unexpected, serendipity, all give the lie to the thought that this world is just one big piece of machinery. People do get better unexpectedly. Christopher Reeve slowly inches back to life after breaking his neck; the Finnish motor racing driver, Mika Hakkinen, recovers after a head injury sustained in a hundred mile an hour head-on crash into the side barriers. It looks as if two things are inseparably intertwined; there is inevitability – this is bound to happen – and there is what we may call 'un-inevitability' – this may or may not happen. Inevitability and un-inevitability are intertwined, part of the same whole, *because that's the way things are.*

The point is that what we call the law of nature, and remember that the laws of nature are now regarded as descriptions of what seems to be the case, includes both possibilities. There are those things that have always happened in certain circumstances. Apples which drop off trees always fall to the ground; that's a law of nature. When the unexpected happens, however, and Superman partially recovers after a terrible horse-riding accident, I believe he is also fulfilling a law of nature; a law which says that some things, particularly where people are involved, are not wholly inevitable. Apparently they can go two ways. Admittedly, the way of regularity and dependableness is more common; but there is another reading of the same law in which the unexpected becomes possible.

All this seems to suggest that things are more open, more porous, than we had expected. Here is Nicholas Negroponte again speaking about the digital world in which reality, in this case information, is reduced to a cluster or series of bits (binary units). What enables the bits, in their compressed form, to add up to pieces of information is the shape of the clusters, the number and frequency of them – and the shape is not only the sum total of the bits themselves but of the spaces in between them:

> Matter is made of atoms. If you could look at the smoothly
> polished metal surface at a subatomic scale, you would see
> mostly holes. It appears smooth and solid because the discreet
> pieces are so small. Likewise digital output.[5]

It is rather like one of those huge colour advertisements you get on roadside hoardings. Examine it closely and what, from a distance looks like a solid field of colour, is in fact made up of dots – pixels – which arrange the available space to form the picture. They do the same on the television screen. So do Monet's brush strokes in that series of gigantic paintings of the water-lilies on the lake at Giverny which arrange the spaces to give the impression of what is there so that, standing back, you say, 'Oh, I can see that!'

Perhaps we inhabit a world with more space in it than we think, which allows the possibility of more connections than the rigid determinist who has reduced everything to unyielding cause and effect will allow. Sometimes, against all the odds a sick person will get better. Life will exercise its as yet unexplained, but in principle explicable, option for life. I am not talking here about the laws of nature being suspended or broken, by the actions of what Paul Davies calls 'the manipulative, organizational God'. The God with whom I am trying to keep faith does not need to be spoken about in that way. The laws do not need to be broken; they already include many options and I have no hesitation in saying that when those options are surrounded by prayer and understood by faith, the outcome will sometimes be called miraculous because it will overwhelm us with its unexpected goodness.

It is not open to us now to know about beginnings or ends, although one day it may be; we simply work with what we have. What we have is a world that is porous and in the natural inter-play between the possibilities, the solids and the spaces, the causes and effects, the ifs and the maybes, there is the life of God, who constantly, through all the long aeons of evolution, is urging on his creation to a purpose, or more probably a multitude of purposes, known only to him, but foreshadowed in the Christ. Just as Darwin realized that what the natural world needed in its evolutionary path was time, so time is needed for the purposes of God to be fulfilled. But in the life and ministry of Jesus time is brought to a single point and in him, briefly, all that God is comes to rest.

4.   Origins

In recent years there has been no tougher critic of religion than the Oxford biologist, Richard Dawkins. In a series of books with titles such as *The Selfish Gene*, *The Blind Watchmaker* and *River out of Eden*, Dawkins has made the Darwinian case for cumulative natural selection as the driving force of all life. No divine hand need be supposed, no supernatural creation is required. The laws of physics and of biology are quite adequate to explain the origins of life and our place within the order of things. Dawkins' inspiration for the title of his second book comes from the eighteenth century theologian, William Paley, who in 1802 published a book, which Dawkins greatly admires, called *Natural Theology – or Evidences of the Existence of the Deity Collected from the Appearances of Nature.* In his opening chapter, Paley says that just as one might infer the presence of a watchmaker from the chance discovery of a watch lying on the ground, so one might also conclude that the natural world with all its complex design must have a maker. It does, says Dawkins, but not one which has planned it all:

> Natural selection, the blind, unconscious, automatic process which Darwin discovered, and which we now know is the explanation for the existence and apparently purposeful form of all life, has no purpose in mind. It has no mind and no mind's eye. It does not plan the future. It has no vision, no foresight, no sight at all. If it can be said to play the role of watchmaker in nature, it is the *blind* watchmaker.[6]

We have become used, in Christian circles, to talking about God as Creator, as the mover of history, as exercising providential care over human beings sometimes to the extent of performing miracles which imply that the normal laws of life have been temporarily suspended. It is, therefore, not actually a bad thing for us to take the force of what Dawkins is saying although it is painful. Look at it this way. Good science can only make for good theology. It should toughen us up, make us more aware of what we are saying, help us realize that we do not have a monopoly on a sense of wonder, which Dawkins has in abundance, or on the search after truth. So what can be said?

1.   I recently asked a biologist, a university teacher, 'Is this, or something very much like it, generally thought to be the right answer?' I was holding a copy of *The Blind Watchmaker* at the time. 'Yes,' he replied without hesitation. Frankly, that's good enough for me. No doubt the professional biologists will want to criticize, correct or fine-tune Richard Dawkins where that is necessary, but it is a fundamental mistake to think that the 'religious' answer has to be different from the scientific answer. As Paul Davies has said, 'It is truly remarkable that religious adherents have not learned the lesson of history that nature can order its own affairs.'[7] There is just one major caveat to that, to which I shall return later.

2.   Dawkins says that living things like the human eye are too improbable in their complexity and too beautifully 'designed' to have come into being through chance. His answer, and Darwin's, is that they are the result of

'gradual, step-by-step transformations from simple beginnings, from primordial entities sufficiently simple to have come into existence by chance'.[8] But once started, the process is anything but chancy; it is in fact a powerful cumulative process driven 'by nonrandom survival'. The grim reaper ensures that living things that have even the slightest edge over their contemporaries survive longer and the accumulation of minute changes speeds the process of adaptation and enables greater and greater complexity to happen. He famously illustrates this with his biomorphs, computer-produced line drawings of recognizable shapes (recognizable only because our eye associates them with a shape we already know) begun from a single line branching in two directions. But, and it is an important but, how does the whole process begin? Where does the first 'line' come from?

At this point we must turn to his chapter headed 'Origins and Miracles'. It was looking at his opening paragraph that persuaded me to keep in the two previous sections. Dawkins begins:

> Chance, luck, coincidence, miracle. One of the main topics of this chapter is miracles and what we mean by them. My thesis will be that events that we commonly call miracles are not supernatural, but are part of a spectrum of more-or-less improbable natural events. A miracle, in other words, if it occurs at all, is a tremendous stroke of luck. Events don't fall neatly into natural events versus miracles.[9]

We are on common ground – almost! Unfortunately, there is neither space nor time here to develop Dawkins' argument about improbable coincidence, save to say that the process of cumulative natural selection has the vast ages of geological time to play with in the search for the one improbable set of coincidences that set the whole process going. Dawkins illustrates two possibilities for that improbable set of circumstances in which the first vital step of replication might have happened, the primeval soup theory and the 'inorganic mineral' theory of the Glasgow chemist Graham Cairns-Smith, the details of which are not necessary for our purpose now. But what is fascinating, given the absolute certainty with which Dawkins talks about the blind watchmaker, is the tentative way in which he now speaks. 'I thought I would fly a kite' for Cairns-Smith, he says[10]; 'Our own subjective judgement' about the origins of life on earth may be wrong 'by a factor of a hundred million'[11] and so on. In fact, his discussion of this ultimate problem, of the circumstances of the first improbability, is decidedly speculative. I am content to realize that the biological reason for life lies somewhere at the end of the road signposted 'Darwin'. We also need to be aware of how many noughts are needed in the odds that make possible the initial spark of self-replicating life and of Richard Dawkins' own quite candid assessment that 'the theory we are looking for has got to be the kind of theory that seems implausible to our limited, Earth-bound, decade-bound imaginations'.[12] What it amounts to, I believe, is that in the face of such a singularity human beings looking for explanations, either religious or non-religious, can only exercise caution and be modest in their claims.

3.   In any case, might it not be a mistake to confuse the origins of something with the 'finished' product or with the process by which it came to be regarded as finished. In Salisbury Methodist Church, there is a large embroidery, four metres wide and five metres deep, the subject of which is *Creation*. It was made by Angela Dewar and Gisela Banbury, two ecclesiastical designers and embroiderers, to mark the re-opening of the church after a long period of refurbishment. Their brief was 'to reflect God's activity in creation and environment, encompassing the physical and spiritual dimensions of human life, and evoking worship'. It depicts the circling planets, the earth with its abundant life, a village with houses tumbling down a hillside and amidst it all, life-giving light with DNA-like spirals emerging here and there to fill the earth and the cosmos. The embroidery is made entirely of silk and is mounted in seven parallel panels on aluminium frames, another way of arranging space so that space in between becomes a part of the whole design. You could trace its origins back to the original silkworms but a lot has happened since. The original silkworms always had the potential, but other things besides silkworms were needed for that potential to be realized. This is not an argument from design; just the modest claim that the finished product is greater than the sum of its parts and different from any one of them.

So also with human beings who share their biology with the rest of the animal kingdom but who, along the way, have been formed, by God I believe, to be people of moral, artistic, scientific and social capability. As a result, human beings can themselves 'create' the world by feats of medicine and technology, by artistic sense, by the sheer skill of language and the giving of names to what otherwise would be nameless and strange, by the offering of care and respect which stirs life in other human beings where perhaps there was only fear and isolation.

I wrote these pages around Christmas time. Three or four days before Christmas we went to the Service of Lessons and Carols in Winchester Cathedral. Walking across the Cathedral Close at the end of the afternoon, we were confronted by the floodlit mass of the old Cathedral, much of it a thousand years old, full of history and of faith. The Cathedral, too, is a hard, empirical fact which deserves an explanation. So also do its builders, when to put even one storey upon another was a triumph; likewise, its preservers through centuries of political and religious turmoil, not to mention its contemporary worshippers who witness to a late century mood which resists the belief that human beings can be reduced to pieces of biological machinery, no matter how wondrous and intricate those pieces might be. Another biologist, Steve Jones, has written:

> It is the essence of all scientific theories that they cannot resolve everything. Science cannot answer the questions that philosophers – or children – ask: why are we here, what is the point of being alive, how ought we to behave? Genetics has almost nothing to say about what makes us more than just machines driven by biology, about what makes us human.[13]

Theology, our thinking about God, also tries to answer those questions. True enough, we may have got it wrong in the past and our thinking still is not up to speed. We have not always engaged with others who have moved in different worlds of knowledge and experience and we have often claimed too much. But that is not the whole picture and now, as we move rapidly through changes and challenges that our predecessors could not have imagined, Christian theologians must act speedily, and intelligibly, to repair the omissions. The problem is that it begins to look like watering things down. That's the criticism so often deployed, both by traditionalists within the church and by those scientific rationalists who are hostile to faith and who prefer a readily identified target. However, I can see no reason at all why our *understanding* of God should not also change. That is not selling out or watering down or any of the other put-downs. It is the deliberate and often painful opening up of a conversation between the tradition of faith and our contemporary knowledge and experience, in the middle of which we might discover our own appropriate way of keeping faith.

I earlier quoted Paul Davies who said that it was a pity religious people did not recognize that nature 'can order its own affairs'. I said there was a caveat. My caveat is this: that so far as nature is concerned, God, as I understand him, has 'emptied' himself into the natural world so that its laws are his ways of being, because those laws, God's laws, are the only ways by which life on this planet is sustainable. The word 'emptied', used in this sense, needs some explanation. It occurs only once in the biblical record, in one of St. Paul's letters where Paul speaks of the Christ Jesus who at his incarnation '*emptied* himself, taking the form of a slave, being born in human likeness'.[14] It was an expression of humility. The Greek word used by Paul is *kenosis* and as Christian scholars tried to use the idea of self-emptying to understand Christ's incarnation, their thinking became known as the kenotic theory. Incidentally, Charles Wesley used kenotic thinking in lines such as:

> He laid his glory by,
>   He wrapped him in our clay;
> Unmarked by human eye,
>   The latent Godhead lay;
> Infant of days he here became,
> And bore the mild Immanuel's name.[15]

One of the questions asked of kenotic theology was this: 'Who is governing the universe while God has laid aside all power but love in the birth of Jesus?' Here precisely we need to invoke Paul Davies but also to go beyond the self-emptying Christ to the self-emptying God. The laws of nature which uphold life are God's laws because he has emptied himself into the beginning, the sustaining, the fulfilling and the perfecting of all things. Richard Dawkins rejects the religious concern about the pain human beings discover in the tragedies of the world; we live in a heartless, cold universe, the morally neutral realm of the blind watchmaker (see Dawkins' *River out of Eden*[16]).

An alternative view is that each human tragedy represents the eternal crucifixion of Christ; each cry of pain finds its echo in his shout of dereliction from the cross; each tiny miracle an improbable – to what Dawkins rightly calls 'our decade-bound imaginations' – fulfilling of natural law rather than a breaking of it, when life has acted graciously towards us, because that is its intent, *and we have recognized it*. To talk about the self-emptying God in the same breath as any of the physical or biological theories about origins appears to me to add no further noughts to the already staggeringly huge improbability of anything existing at all.

And it is a kinder view. By that I mean that in God we might come to see the world, not as a hostile place in which we must kick and scratch to get our own way or to protect our own from harm. Many see it that way already. There is a brutal streak in all of us and our ways of organizing things will reflect that brutality if that is the best way we know. That is one of the reasons, perhaps the chief, why we need the path of redemption. But we are also in touch with other ways, drawing inspiration at other wells, which speak of the nobility of being human, of our ability for self-giving on a grand scale for which there is no reward, no evolutionary payback. Such generosity is a reflection of the generosity of God.

5.   Are we getting ahead of God?

This was the subject I was given to speak about one Sunday last year in the wake of two newspaper stories, one about a fifty-nine year old woman reported to have given birth to twins after receiving fertility treatment in Italy, the other about a black woman being implanted with the eggs of a white woman. There was also at the time some discussion about the possibility, no more than that, of using ovarian tissue from aborted human foetuses to produce mature eggs which might be capable of being fertilized to produce a baby. It is now eighteen years since the birth of the world's first test-tube baby but the fact is that this approach is only about fifteen per cent successful and many couples try again and again at great expense. There are now about twenty different ways to have a baby. So the issues raised are enormously important.

As a result of the Warnock Report in 1984, controls were put in place and the Human Fertilization and Embryology Authority was established. It has twenty-one members, some of whom are medical people, some members of the general public. As well as looking at the science involved, its task is to assess the mood of the public, what is generally acceptable and what is not. Mary Warnock added as a postscript to her report that the law should be brought up to date, 'so that society may be protected from its real and very proper fear of a rudderless voyage into unknown and threatening waters'.

At the same time other genetic possibilities raise both opportunities and problems. There are some fifty proposals now being considered by Britain's ethics committee on gene therapy, some of which might mean the use of a genetically engineered virus to stimulate a patient's immune system to attack a particular disease. Professor Karol Sikora, a specialist at the Royal Postgraduate Medical School at the Hammersmith Hospital, was quoted in *The*

Independent newspaper in January 1995 as saying that 'by the end of the decade, some form of gene therapy will be routinely available in hospitals throughout the world'.[17]

Are we then getting ahead of God as some people fear? It all depends upon our view of God. We drew ahead of the vengeful, whimsical, all-powerful demon of a god twenty centuries ago, in Jesus. We left behind the simplistic puppetmaster of a god who pulls all the strings two or three centuries ago, with the rise of modern science; likewise the old man in the sky, as people like John Robinson taught us a different way of thinking. But who can get ahead of the God who is constantly creating and recreating through the very natural processes which run through the universe as its life? The Christian understanding is of a God who constantly draws men and women to seek a better life, a more fulfilled life, a more compassionate life. That means we must take full responsibility in the search for what is genuinely humane. Those who are at the leading edge of research into life itself and the means by which it might be enhanced are primary agents in that.

From the perspective of those who are trying to keep faith with God, what are the gains of cutting free from the old sterile arguments between science and religion and continuing an open conversation instead?

1. The first thing that should be said is that if, for example, in the field of human origins, Darwin or something much like Darwinism got it right, there is nothing at all to be gained by denying it or by constantly looking for the flaws. The truth is liberating. It frees people of faith within the human community, or at least those competent to do so, to get on and share with others the very urgent tasks of understanding the causes of disease, famine and the degradation of the environment and to do something about them. These, and the profound ambiguity of science, technology and industrialization in their uses by human beings for good or ill, were amongst the critical questions requiring a faith for the third millennium according to Hans Küng, as we saw earlier.

2. An open conversation will also help strengthen the moral framework of choice within which the debate about the uses of science and technology can take place. The early chapters of Genesis, so easily misunderstood if the atmosphere between science and faith is bad, sets two stories side by side in a quite postmodern kind of way. One suggests that humanity is made in the image of God, full of his goodness and creative energy, the other says that

human beings are made from the dust of the earth, part of the clay, the root and the rock of the soil we tread on. Yet this highly ambiguous being has the ability to choose between right and wrong, to go in search of knowledge and to find out where the limits are. The irony of this combination of the divine image and dust of the earth should not be lost on us. We can use it to test our limits, to realize the responsibilities that properly belong to us.

3.   There is, finally, the enormous gain of finding that we are part of a common journey of understanding that will tell us about our origins, about our place in the universe – probably a very small one – and about our ultimate destiny. It is reported that astronomers studying new photographs of deep space from the Hubble telescope are being forced 'to abandon the language of scientific precision and to speak only of "wonderment"'.[18] Why? Because the image showed more than one thousand five hundred galaxies, each one of which might contain one hundred billion suns all streaming away from the earth at nineteen thousand miles per second. The light from the dimmest of those galaxies set off on its journey about twelve to fifteen billion years ago. For some that wonderment will not lead to God. They will have their own response which will in turn inspire their science. Others will make the same journey and read the map differently, discovering everywhere the signs of the presence of God. Perhaps the deciding factor of whether or not faith is a real option for some people will not finally be their knowledge of God in the natural world but their experience of God in their personal lives. The one interprets, informs the other. To one aspect of that, redemption, we must now turn.

6. 'NOTHING IS BEYOND REDEMPTION'

1. Recognition and hope

'Resume? I can't remember my life. I wouldn't know where to look for it.'

'You musn't talk in this way.' Jeanne was angry. Her pale skin showed, for the first time since Stephen had known her, a pin-point of blood in the cheeks. With her left hand she lightly beat the wooden bench on which they were sitting to emphasize what she said.

'Of course you won't resume whatever it was you were doing in Paris, drifting around as a carpenter or whatever it was. You'll do something better, you'll do something worthwhile.'

Stephen turned his eyes slowly to her. 'You're a dear woman, Jeanne. I would do what you say. But it's not the details of a life I've lost. It's the reality itself.'

Jeanne's eyes filled with tears. 'Then we must make it come back. I'll bring it back for you. I'll help you to find whatever it is you have lost. Nothing is beyond redemption.'[1]

We are in France. The year is 1918 and the war is almost at an end. Stephen Wraysford has been at the front from the beginning. He has seen the most terrifying things, gone into fighting and carnage so appalling that after one particular advance the chaplain threw away his cross in despair. It is still not quite over. There will be one more horror – and resurrection of a kind. Through it all Stephen has carried his own wound, the memory of Jeanne's sister Isabelle and their child whom he has never seen. With curious irony, Stephen's war is fought around Amiens, the very place where he and Isabelle first met. It was there at her home where they heard the birds singing outside in the garden. Only as Sebastian Faulk's fine book, *Birdsong*, nears its end and time begins to slip-slide, forwards and backwards, do you realize that the story is being told, the details recalled and also the reality, not just for Stephen's redemption but for someone else's too. At the end, there is birdsong, 'to be heard by those still living'. We also become aware that the longed – for redemption, and what healing there is, comes because we have gone over the ground, as it were; the story has been re-called for us, and if it seems that there have been pauses here and there, that is because it has been

67

painstakingly pieced together by someone we only get to know late on, someone for whom it all matters.

Perhaps we should not think it strange that, in a century which has included such great wars and so much suffering, we find that at its end one of the great metaphors carrying the hopes of redemption should be the Great War itself, because many people regard that war as the beginning of the twentieth century proper. Now, writers like Sebastian Faulks and Pat Barker with her Booker prize winner, *The Ghost Road*, find their own kind of resolution through events that happened eighty years ago, before most of us were born but still close enough for some people, the very oldest within our communities, to bear testimony. The Great War, with its pictures of shattered landscapes and its aching poetry, has become a vehicle which carries our own anxiety and the sense of uncertainty which follows the destruction, in our own times, of familiar territory and old certainties.

The landscape which we know best, and of which we are becoming increasingly afraid, is the modern city. It is not surprising, therefore, when the city becomes the metaphor for our fear and lack of confidence in so many contemporary films; films like Martin Scorsese's *Casino*, Kathryn Bigelow's *Blue Steel* and *Strange Days*, and Ridley Scott's classic, *Blade Runner*. In Michael Mann's film *Heat*, Robert De Niro plays the criminal, Neil McCauley, whose watchword is never to get into something from which he can't walk away in thirty seconds. Does that represent a tenable, even fashionable attitude, in the postmodern Nineties? The film takes almost three hours to answer the question as he and the policeman, Vincent Hanna (Al Pacino) lead parallel lives in which good and bad seem strangely mixed. It is a violent film set in Los Angeles with its entrancing night skyline. Whether or not the violence, or its perpetrators, can be redeemed depends upon your view of the human relationships portrayed in the film.

By contrast, the wilderness of ice and snow is the unlikely and redeeming alternative to the crowded, frantic life of the modern city in E. Annie Proulx's book, *The Shipping News*. The central character is Brooklyn-born Quoyle – do we ever get to know his first name? – who, 'At thirty-six, bereft, brimming with grief and thwarted love . . . steered away to Newfoundland, the rock that generated his ancestors, a place he had never been or thought to go.'[2] There amongst the boats and bad weather, Quoyle writes the shipping column for the local newspaper and finds his own kind of resolution. A sub-continent away, David Guterson's deliciously titled *Snow Falling on Cedars* is set in the Fifties in an isolated island community north of Seattle – does that sound familiar to film-goers? – in Washington State. It, too, is about a newspaper man and the aftermath of war, the war between Japan and the United States.[3]

This deliberate getting-away-from-the-city setting is all very different from the four *Rabbit* books of John Updike in which Harry 'Rabbit' Angstrom never stops running but is rarely far from his home-town of 'Mt Judge, suburb of the city of Brewer, fifth largest city in Pennsylvania'. We first hear of him in the Fifties, now a fashionable cultural decade, before he becomes a salesman in his father-in-law's Toyota car lot and he lives long enough to see the introduction of the new Lexus cars – Updike's signal of the new world he saw approaching at the end of the Eighties. In every sense Rabbit belongs to the second half of the twentieth century but hardly to the Nineties or beyond. So round about nineteen-eighty-something Rabbit is finally '*At Rest*'. His son, Nelson, pleads with him: 'Don't die, Dad, don't! . . .' 'Well Nelson,' he says, 'all I can tell you is, it isn't so bad.' Rabbit thinks he should maybe say more, the kid looks wildly expectant, but enough. Maybe. Enough.'[4]

Is it dying that 'isn't so bad'? Or is that also Harry Angstrom's verdict on life, his life, and perhaps constitutes a kind of redemption in the face of the mistakes he has made and the tangle in which he and others have often found themselves?

We do not often interpret redemption in quite this way. Redemption is a religious word, a biblical word. It surely has to do with what we call the saving work of Christ, about sin, repentance, Sankey and Moody. But when we talk about 'redemption' we need to remember where the word comes from. Its background is far from pretty:

> It is derived from the practice of buying back something which formerly belonged to the purchaser, but has for some reason passed out of his possession (as in redeeming a pledge from pawn) or of paying the price required to secure a benefit (the money paid for acquiring or freeing a slave) and comes from the same root as the word ransom.[5]

Slave market, pawnshop, commercialism and money make up the rather commonplace, seedy, environment out of which religion conjures one of its finest words. That is why I hold on to the view that redemption lies close to the heart of the everyday and cannot easily be separated from the places where we live our ordinary lives. Writers, painters, dramatists, film-makers and many others all have their own vision of the shape redemption might take. Sometimes, it is recognizably religious. Often it is a mere glimpse of the nobility of the human spirit or of the questioning of the human mind or even a burst of laughter which Peter Berger once called a 'signal of transcendence'.[6]

The striking thing about books and films is that they are a re-playing of the story, a going over of the ground which to some extent is shared ground with us, the audience. Their powerfulness, if they have any, is in their ability to resonate with our own experience and emotions and to generate not simply pleasure but hope. It is in that sense that I want to say that they are redemptive. Neither do they lack that dimension that many people would say is essential in any drama of redemption, that of transcendence. Robert Redford's film, *A River Runs Through It*, begins in a sepia light that is almost too dark to see by; it moves through the brilliant colours of the Montana Rockies and closes once more in the gathering dusk as the old Norman Maclean still casts his line on the Big Blackwater River. We hear him saying:

> Eventually, all things merge into one, and a river runs through it. The river was cut by the world's great flood and runs over rocks from the basement of time. On some of the rocks are timeless raindrops. Under the rocks are the words, and some of the words are theirs.
> I am haunted by waters.[7]

The film is the old man's recollection of his early life, of his Presbyterian minister father whose verdict on Methodists was that 'they were Baptists who could read', of a devoted mother and the enigma of a younger brother, played by Brad Pitt. In some ways, it is the story of the Prodigal Son but in reverse. The older brother goes away to get his education and returns to find that his younger brother, who has stayed at home, is a lost soul. The great sadness of the film is that their father only communicates with the older brother when he is reciting Wordsworth or preaching from the pulpit, and with both his sons when they go fishing for trout together. We watch the younger boy, who when he is fishing has almost heroic qualities, gradually slipping beyond their reach despite their care and love.

It is this quality of going over the ground once more, almost looking for the redemptive moment of recognition and hope which may be missed, what David Tracy would call the manifestation of truth through conversation, that I

70

want to reflect upon. In the world of literature, theatre and film we see the possibilities of going over the ground. Jung believed that each of his patients had a secret story, the uncovering of which was the key to any treatment.[8] Perhaps individuals and even whole societies need to discover their secret stories, the hidden scripts of their lives, before any real healing can take place. The human story can be endlessly re-visited, re-interpreted, understood afresh. My point here is that there is the hint of a correspondence between its constant re-telling and a certain New Testament way of presenting humanity's redemption by God. It is a correspondence that I wish to take seriously because it offers a context of meaning in which both can be interpreted. To understand it we need to return to the early centuries of the Christian Faith.

2.   Recapitulation

In 177 CE a severe persecution broke out in Lyons in which the bishop, Pothinus, was martyred at the age of ninety. When it had all died down, Irenaeus became the new bishop. He had come to Gaul some years earlier but had been in Rome at the time of the persecution. Irenaeus was born in Smyrna in Asia Minor, possibly as early as 120. He claims to have been taught by his bishop, Polycarp, who according to tradition had known John, the Lord's disciple. Throughout his life, Irenaeus had been concerned with at least two heresies, gnosticism and docetism. The gnostics claimed that salvation was through some special knowledge, gnosis, brought to the world by Jesus to which only the initiated were privy; the docetists believed that Jesus was not a human being at all because God could not possibly be enthralled by our flesh. In other words, both heresies represented an underlying and determined strand in religious thought that says that redemption is a privileged affair for the few and certainly has nothing to do with the earthiness of the world or of our human nature. It was to make it quite clear that Christianity will have none of this that the writer of the Fourth Gospel says that the Word became flesh. It was in his writings against these heresies that Irenaeus developed his doctrine of recapitulation. For him redemption was located precisely in the life and death of Jesus. Put briefly, he said that what Adam, the first human being, lost through disobedience, Jesus, the second Adam, gained for us by his obedience. Irenaeus wrote, 'Because of his measureless love, he became what we are in order to enable us to become what he is.'[9]

Of course, he took his cue from St. Paul who said, 'For just as by the one man's disobedience the many were made sinners, so by the one man's obedience the many will be made righteous' (Romans 5:19). For this idea to have any credibility at all, both Paul and Irenaeus depended upon a belief that in the first Adam the whole human race was potentially present.[10] Irenaeus' idea of recapitulation sounded very archaic when I first came across it as a young theological student round about 1960. I knew about the ancient Hebrew idea that one person could embody a nation's spirit and destiny, but that was old stuff, the result of a primitive and limited mind. Now the geneticist, Steve Jones, tells me 'that each gene is a message from our forebears and together they contain the whole story of evolution'.[11]

Moreover, for a variety of reasons, there is now much more to the notion of human solidarity than we could ever have guessed. Solidarity has a resonance in our minds which acts as the counterbalance to the 'me culture' and says something very important about what human beings are meant to be. As Timothy Gorringe has put it in a stimulating exposition of atonement as the educating work of the Spirit throughout history: 'Because human beings only exist in complex patterns of social relationships they can only be redeemed in those patterns.'[12] If that is true, it underlines the importance of keeping our understanding of creation and redemption together. The verbal collage of where we are at the end of the twentieth century that I tried to construct earlier is not an optional extra. It is a description, no matter how inadequate, of the world which is being brought to birth through the patient creating, redeeming work of God.

I have left many gaps in my description of Irenaeus' doctrine of recapitulation, but my aim has been to sketch out an idea from the early years of Christian thinking about the way in which the life of Jesus is significant for the redemption of humanity. For me, coming at the problem through film and literature as I have attempted to do in this instance, the crucial point is that Jesus has gone over the ground and summed up all things in himself. As we look upon his life and teaching with understanding and respond with committed lives, we share in his redemptive hope.

Serious film-making is not simply playing out fantasy. It, too, reflects my verbal collage in a continually changing and surprising fashion. One of its recurring themes, for example, is the relationship between human beings and the machine. It is often asking questions about the interplay of good and evil; it tests our own moral reactions; it exposes emotions that we keep under control at other times. But, of course, film-making has its limits. For all its ability to expose, to re-play the story of our humanity and to interrogate us as

72

well as entertain, we know that somehow there is a disjunction between the film and us. We know that we see only the surface. The film is mostly just a thin section of a larger whole, a whole for which the film makers cannot or will not be responsible. The director will give you that message in the final scene before the credits roll. No matter how inspired or taken out of ourselves we have been, we know that at the end we must return to our own lives in all their complexity, where the consequences of our actions cannot be avoided by switching to another scene. A film might tell us that humanity can be redeemed but it does not, of itself, redeem.

3.   Redemptive Suffering

The theme to which art and literature in all their forms continually return is the enigma of being human, of being mortal and prone to accident, cruelty and perversity and yet having a potential for nobility and self-sacrifice. The very greatest art and literature continue to question us years, centuries even, after it was first conceived. No one who has seen the 'Moses' of Michelangelo in the church of San Pietro in Vincoli in Rome can quite erase the memory of those horns, that enigmatic expression, that entangling of the right hand in the flowing beard that signify – what? Was this really the angry reaction of Moses as he returned from Sinai to discover the people worshipping the Golden Calf, or was Michelangelo re-writing the Exodus story, as Freud supposed, and Moses was portrayed in the very act of trying to save the stone tablets of the law from crashing to the ground?[13] As we engage in such a conversation, so we begin to confront the enigmas within ourselves.

Great art and literature frequently return to the ambiguities of being human, of how we are capable of both the good and the evil. It is the human capacity for evil with which we have increasingly had to come to terms as the century has gone on. This was the great moral jolt delivered by the wars of this century, the symbol of which has become the Holocaust. At the heart of all of us there is the propensity for something far more terrible than we had guessed. There is no need to invent supernatural explanations for it. That is merely to throw off responsibility. How does a responsible faith deal with the human capacity for evil? It says two things and at its best, those two things are enacted. It confronts evil with the redemptive power of sacrificial suffering and it overcomes evil by the redemptive power of committed action.

I have a sense of treading on holy ground as I read again the following prayer. It was found in one of the camps in 1945.

> Remember, Lord, not only the men and women of goodwill
> but also those of ill will.
> But do not only remember all the suffering
> they have inflicted on us.
> Remember the fruits we bought, thanks to this suffering –
> our comradeship, our loyalty, our humility,
> the courage, the generosity, the greatness of heart
> which has grown out of all this.
> And when they come to judgement
> let all the fruits that we have borne
> be their forgiveness.
>
> (Ravensbruck)

I think I hear through those words, which only the sufferer in those circumstances has the right to utter, the belief that human sinfulness and all its effects can be borne redemptively for others; that the worst of which we are capable is not actually enough to defeat the goodness and forgiveness of God expressed through gracious and faithful lives. They are the words of someone who had centuries of prayer behind them, someone for whom Isaiah's description of the one 'wounded for our transgressions' (Isaiah 53:5) were second nature. We can put out of our minds the primitive idea of sacrifice demanded by an angry God. This is the self-offering of faith, the light shining in the darkness which the darkness cannot extinguish. For Christian people, the embracing by Christ of his cross has become the sign of God's presence in suffering and in the continual struggle against the inhumanity of which we are all capable and for which we need to be forgiven. We also see in it the most powerful expression of a gracious God for whom all things can be redeemed. Nothing is beyond redemption as Jeanne, the long-neglected but ultimately redeeming older sister, says to Stephen Wraysford. Thus the not-quite-final-word in the drama of human redemption is, 'Father forgive'. Why is that the not-quite-final-word? Because the last word, in this world at least, is the always-possible human 'No.'

4.   Redemptive obedience

How is redemption real-ized and given practical shape in life? For Irenaeus, obedience was crucial.   Jesus, by his obedience, reversed the effects of humanity's disobedience; now, as a result, we can share in his redemption by our obedience to God. I recognize that obedience is now a difficult word. It may be especially so for women, as Mary Grey has pointed out. Too often, she says, women have been told to be submissive and to achieve salvation through self-denying service and attitudes.[14] However, the obedience that I have in mind is not that sort of crushing obedience which diminishes people, jumping to when we hear God's voice. It is the sort of obedience that seeks to work with the grain in the wood rather than against it, to co-operate with the divine purpose rather than contest and frustrate it. Paul said, 'Let the same mind be in you that was in Christ Jesus . . .' (Philippians 2:5).

I have on my bookshelves two books by the Methodist scholar, Robert F. Wearmouth. One of them has the title *The Social and Political Influence of Methodism in the Twentieth Century*. I recall Wearmouth's books at this moment for one reason. He was concerned to record the contribution in committed, obedient lives of ordinary people as he found them in the minutiae of local government, trade unions and voluntary societies. There are many pages of short paragraphs, mostly one sentence in length. For example, on a page from the chapter headed' Methodism and Local Government Service', you find: William Pit, a checkweighman and member of Stanley Urban District Council;   Matthew G. Armstrong, a pioneer of local government administration;   Robert Thomas Batey, 'quiet, reserved and dignified';   John W. Beckham, interested in the welfare of the aged; Mrs Elizabeth Brass, a pioneer of women's movements and Chairman of the Council.[15]

I find Wearmouth's catalogue of otherwise forgotten, committed lives rather moving. It is a vivid reminder of the redemptive character of people's lives. They believed that they could build a new Jerusalem here and, if that turned out to be more than a little difficult, they would at least improve things as much as they could. They proved the truth of Blake's dictum that 'he who would do good, must do it in minute particulars'.

Jim Wallis, of the Sojourners Community in Washington, is making the same point in his *The Soul of Politics*. He offers a fairly bleak picture of a society that is not working, but there is an alternative:

We need to articulate clearly the essential moral character of the many crises we confront, the connections between them, and the choices we must make. By being faithful to a moral vision of politics in our own lives and communities, we will make our best contribution and offer our most profound participation. The little islands of hope we create are harbingers of a different political future for our countries.[16]

The second part of his book records the stories of individuals or small groups who offer 'signs of transformation' within their communities, often at the margins. Not for him the so-called moral majority, the use of the state's power to assert Christian values, or at least one view of Christian values. Instead he paints a different picture, of the renewal both of individuals and communities by the patient work of humble Christian men and women. I think there are two things here. The first is that in all our communities there are people, sometimes from different faiths and sometimes from none, who work for transformation. They stand alongside families under stress, people who have no work, young people whose lives are empty, couples whose relationship has broken down, people who are homeless or who are the victims of crime. Their sense of obedience to a particular vision, their sheer commitment to it in terms of life and work, is redemptive.

Perhaps in the end their achievement is small. That is testimony to the hardness of the rock of injustice and insensitivity which they have been struggling to break. Nevertheless, in the particularity of their hopefulness, they have witnessed to a light which the darkness has not extinguished. If they have lit one small light which has played around the truth of human dignity and God's eternal presence with the world, they have served their turn.

The second aspect of obedience is the willingness of individual people to regard their life's work as a vocation. There are no restrictions on what can be regarded as vocational because it is not so much a question of the type of work we do as our willingness to offer it in the service of God and others, and through that offering, to discover our true selves. David Clark, of the Christians in Public Life Programme puts it this way:

– We are called to be partners with God in his continuing work of creation within the personal, corporate and global spheres of life.

- We are called to be partners with Christ as he frees and empowers individuals, institutions and nations to fulfil their God-given possibilities.
- We are called to be partners with the Spirit as she works for justice, peace and the unity of humankind.

- We are called to be partners with all those who work to further human dignity within the bounds of our common humanity.[17]

Here is a call, literally a *vocation*, to a way of life which goes beyond the bounds of the visible, organized church. It throws down the barriers between sacred and secular. It can be embraced by people of faith and by people of no faith. It is redemptive because it offers an alternative vision to Wordsworth's despairing 'Getting and spending, we lay waste our powers.'[18]

What is more, a reclaiming of a sense of vocation restores our relationship with nature and through nature, with God. As the century closes, one hears repeated calls for a new way of being in relation to nature, one that is not exploitative or based on domination and waste. Those are now coming to be regarded as old attitudes but they will die hard. Men and women working with a vocational view of their lives, however, seeking to restore the damaged fibres of partnership with one another and with the natural world, will offer a counter-cultural perspective which will, itself, be redeeming.

5.   Summing things up

I have come increasingly to see that no single understanding of redemption is adequate all the time. None of them 'works' in every set of circumstances because of the complexity of human need and because of the capacity of God to respond to that need in surprising ways.

For much of my ministry I have embraced what might be called the so-called liberal view that the language of sacrifice was impossibly primitive and that the most helpful understanding of the atonement lay along the road of human beings responding to the forgiving love of God in Christ. Sacrificing to placate an angry God was not part of my theological world. How can you give God human emotions like anger, or picture him as an offended monarch? I still can't, because the more I describe God in human terms, the more I have to picture, to locate God somewhere. The rational part of me cries out against this and, therefore, I continue to struggle with the idea of kenosis as a way of understanding God's presence; God's self-emptying into life and into creation.

And yet, and yet, who will hear the cry of the victim in this or any other century when it falls on deaf human ears if not God? Shall not God be justifiably angry? Anything less would be all too human. But now the language of sacrifice takes on a new twist. What has the power to put things right is not the hapless, sacrificial lamb presented by the uncaring, the wicked laughing things off by a casual offering. Suddenly, everything is changed when the victim, Himself, Herself, Themselves, step(s) forward in the agony of dereliction and says, 'let all the fruits that we have borne be their forgiveness'.

That illuminates for me the one, perfect sacrifice of Christ as few things have done. The Christ who is every woman, every man, by obedience freely given has changed things for ever. Through Christ human beings can receive divine forgiveness and the sign of that is the cross. There is a deep-seated human need to know forgiveness – some would say peace or wholeness – for our half-lived, fragmentary, damaged lives. We are held back from understanding how the notion of sacrifice can help us because in our literalist manner we want to know to whom the sacrifice is being made. But that is to misuse the language of sacrifice we find in the New Testament. As Frances Young has argued, that language had already been 'torn from its pagan roots' in the service of Old Testament religion and been changed in the process.[19] God was not generally thought of as the recipient of a placatory sacrifice. Instead the prophetic voice insisted that justice and righteousness were the desirable offerings. Even in the New Testament reference to sacrifice in St. Paul's writings (Romans 3:25) which is most hotly disputed, it is questionable whether Jesus is the purgation of our sins (expiation) or the placatory sacrifice for our sins (propitiation) – God is not the one to whom the sacrifice is made. On the contrary, God steps forward in Jesus to take the responsibility for putting things right.

I do not think there is a reasonable explanation for what is happening here because we are operating at this point on a deeply sub-conscious level, the level of the shadows that flit across our hidden lives. At the half-understood level of personal anguish and collective guilt, the Christ who goes over the ground of our humanity and takes responsibility is a God-send. But what is crucial to an understanding of New Testament faith is that the responsibility is handed back. We are not infantilized, relieved of the responsibility of being mature human beings. We are invited to take back the responsibility for our lives and our actions in our own self-offering, freely given. That self-offering is the worship of committed, obedient lives.[20] Paul can say:

> I appeal to you therefore, brothers and sisters, by the mercies
> of God, to present your bodies as a living sacrifice, holy and
> acceptable to God, which is your spiritual worship.
>
> (Romans 12:1)

Against all my instincts, then, I need to weave in the idea of sacrifice with the other elements of redemption, the power of self-understanding and catharsis through film, drama and literature, the patient redeeming purpose of committed and obedient people through time, expressing their faith through work and worship. Just as earlier I tried to construct a verbal collage of the different ways of understanding where we are in the late twentieth century, each layer of which will connect with a particular truth within its own frame of reference, but will only be partially true, so we need constantly to hold together different perspectives on redemption, each of which requires the others for the sake of completion. Just as a doctor will have a whole armoury of modern medicine, some of it very powerful indeed, with which to treat the patient and will choose from it the treatment which is appropriate, so the different perspectives on redemption will be appropriate to different people. At different stages in our lives, or in other circumstances, we will feel the power of one understanding, then another to give shape, to renew, to redeem.

Some post-moderns are rather scornful of what they call 'wholeness hunger', that is the search after an understanding which holds everything together. I can understand their reserve. There is too much complexity and sheer diversity to be able to impose single understandings except by abusing people and power. That way lies totalitarianism either in religion or politics. I can live with irony and contradiction. Indeed, I can actually thrive on the ability of language, in poetry and plays, to expose, to shock, to play with meanings and question my too easily acquired certainties. That does not mean, however, that all we have left are disconnected fragments which are meaningless. Here and there, I hear people using the metaphor of weaving, gathering up the fragments, with all its undertones of difference and inclusion. It is perhaps a notion within which Irenaeus himself might have felt at home, with his belief in the Christ who holds all things together, summing them up, and by doing so redeeming them from eternal frustration and meaningless.

7. THE LAND OF UNLIKENESS

1. In the Land of Unlikeness

Only coincidentally does the Land of Unlikeness have anything to do with the millennium. The fact is that in the last half dozen years or so, a number of different streams have begun to converge. The removal of the old East-West divide, and the suddenness of it all, meant that a western way of life built upon the possibility of nuclear threat could take a new turn, although I would be cautious about writing the epitaph of communism too soon. Old conflicts suddenly appeared capable of resolution; South Africa became emblematic of the hopes for peace in many other places. The European Union has become a reality, though quite where it is going is not clear. The so-called tiger economies of East Asia are increasingly held up as models. Once it was Germany, now it is Singapore, South Korea or Taiwan. On the whole, we are better housed, better fed, better clothed, better educated, better informed than we have ever been and we live longer. Hi-tech medicine delivers modern miracles, new hips, new hearts, new drugs capable of relieving conditions that once were incurable. Then there is the new technology, computers, information technology, digitalization and miniaturization. Even now, we are scarcely at the beginning of the revolution that Alvin Toffler, a decade ago, called 'the Third Wave'.

But with all this there is great anxiety although, of course, that is a very Western perspective. Work for many people has been one of the casualties, either because there isn't any or because the job they are doing makes increasing demands and is not always more satisfying. The global economy and new technology are ambiguous. They are capable of bringing enormous long-term benefits but in the meantime many thousands, millions, are having to bear the short-term costs – which might prove to be for the rest of a working life – in an unjust fashion. At the very time that we are coping with new technology, we are beginning to have serious worries about technology in general, about the motor car and energy and the destruction of habitats. To compound our worries, the whole concept of the provision of communal welfare in a modern state is thrown into the melting pot – health, social services, old age – because populations are getting older and, we are told, the cake is not big enough. After thinking that all would be well right through to the grave, we now discover that the rules have changed and that is profoundly disturbing.

Now, the debate is turning to values and goals, inevitable once the ground under our feet begins to shift, as it did in the second half of the Eighties. The arguments are joined, often in simplistic terms, about how we educate our children and students, how we treat those who break the law, how we build our cities and towns, where we shop and how we seek our leisure, the desirability of cutting taxes and the morality of raising them in the first place. Many of the arguments centre around the family and the nature of stable relationships. We fear the effects upon society of divorce. Crime of all sorts, especially violence and drug-related crime, and their portrayal in the media, make it seem to some that society is in terminal decline.

There are choices to be made in politics, some would say unclear choices. Do we wish to be an enterprise capital, a stakeholder democracy or shall we practise partnership politics? Does it really matter any more? Does nation-statehood have a future, or does the future lie in huge trading and political blocs or even with the strong city – 'the hundred mile city', as Deyan Sudjic, architecture correspondent of *The Guardian* describes it, because the 'force-field' or area of influence around the modern city is of those proportions.[1] In any case, can governments make that much difference when, for instance, huge tides of international capital move around the world in cyberspace, putting national economic policies at hazard and for no other ethical purpose than earning a profit? It is because of the limitations on the power of individual governments, and the size of the task confronting them, that Will Hutton suggests that governments in the future will need partners outside Parliament; 'the politics of pluralism', he calls it[2]; Hamish McRae says we will have to get used to the idea that governments will be weak, not because voters deliberately elect weak governments 'but because that is the nature of the world at the close of this century'.[3] Perhaps that is why, when some politicians earlier this year called for their salaries to be doubled, they were greeted with derision, undeserved in my view and deeply damaging to our commonalty, but a sign of the public's present scepticism about the politicians' ability to deliver. In Britain we see a large number of MPs intending to leave Parliament at the next election; the same is true of the United States' Senate and House of Representatives. This may all be temporary but it sits oddly with the end of history and the triumph of liberal democracy.

Internationally, 'the new world order' that was hailed by all just a few years ago with the demise of the USSR and the emergence of new, but frail, democracies in eastern Europe together with joint international fire-fighting to try to resolve several small regional conflicts, met an uncomfortable challenge in the former Yugoslavia. In the end the efforts at peace-keeping by the United Nations, willed by the international community but rarely adequately supported, were portrayed in the press as being swept aside by a strong Nato. For four years we have witnessed ethnic cleansing and atrocities, not in some faraway place, but in Europe. The war correspondent, Jon Swain, recently wrote:

> Wars for me were always abroad – in faraway places where the sun shone and the people were always exotic. That was part of the intoxicating appeal of reporting them; the violence of war among the beauty has trapped many a foreign correspondent's soul. It certainly trapped mine.
>
> Even sad, beautiful Cambodia stole the heart away. Bosnia though, is the heart of darkness. I thought it was inconceivable ever to perceive atrocities of such a scale in Europe. To come here from the prosperity of southeast Asia, whose wars are mercifully over, is to turn the world on its head.[4]

What is more, the Pacific Rim, East Asia as we now call it to reflect our changed perspective on the world map – no longer are things seen to be near or far from us – is not simply the *economic* miracle it has been recently portrayed to be, with China the great awaking market giant. Realpolitik begins to rear its head once more. The emergence of China as a superpower, its stance in relation to Taiwan and Hong Kong, the future of the alliance between Japan and the United States, the discussions in Australia about whether its ties are with the old world or with the new nations of the Pacific, the tension between North and South Korea across the demilitarized zone which has kept them apart since 1953, all indicate that the management of international relations is as crucially important as ever, especially when they are mixed with the vast billions of the global market place.

All in all, despite the huge potential for human well-being in the modern world, I find it difficult to imagine that at any point in the twentieth century there has been a time of greater questioning and worrying about the base line, the common assumptions, of our way of doing things. Perhaps the only comparable decade was the Thirties, with its economic upheaval and growing threat of war. Increasingly, I grow to respect the nerve and courage of my parents' generation. Perhaps, in part, they were sustained by a faith in society's institutions which seems to be denied to many today.

I have tried, in a very scattered way, to give some account of the different streams that have begun to come together in the last six or seven years. Of course, they are fragmentary and the timescale is open to question. They represent for me aspects of the Land of Unlikeness, the shape of which we cannot fully see yet, and probably will never see, because it will be constantly changing. The pace of that change will accelerate; I have absolutely no doubt about that. A new century, a new millennium, might act as a psychological spur to our thinking about the ways by which we shall meet the challenges, no more. It gives us a rare point of reference around which we can arrange our ideas; but, effectively, the twenty-first century has already begun.

2.   A generation of surfers

We belong to a surfing generation in which many people are trying desperately hard to maintain their balance and keep their lives generally heading in the right direction. I use the notion of surfing in a rather more positive way than Richard Hoggart who begins his recent look at *The Way We Live Now* (1995) with a hefty side-swipe at the wave of relativism which he says has risen to a new level in our present, prosperous society. By relativism he means the refusal to make moral judgements or to have standards of quality and the willingness to change the definition of what is right according to how it suits us. He puts it down to a loss of authority at all levels, both religious and lay, a loss that has been perceptible for more than a century, but which has accelerated in the last fifty years. In the end, he seems to relent, however, and points to 'a remarkable moral decency, at all social levels'.[5]

Amongst Richard Hoggart's conclusions, one has particular relevance to my purpose here and reflects a continuing anxiety. He writes:

> The end-of-the-century world of the developed societies has, increasingly, no sanctities, no firm holds. All is successive, momentary, two-dimensional, with little background in a recognised, a recovered, a usable past; no roots. It can therefore have no future or a vision of the future . . .
> Not much more than a generation back the idea of progress, of a progressive amelioration of the human condition, lay somewhere at the back of people's minds, even at the backs of many poor people's minds. It is there no longer. Yet that does not imply a fatalism or disappointment; it implies a living in the successive-present.[6]

Is this what is meant by a so-called 'value-free society', the paralysis of our sense of direction? The twentieth century has taught us that we cannot any longer be confident that every day and in every way we are getting better. Are we, then, as Richard Hoggart suggests, becoming content to live in the 'successive-present', always looking for the new, but for ever staying in the same place, neither disappointed nor regretful that things should not be otherwise, but simply contented, so that the very notions of progress and of caring overmuch about other people's misfortune have been discarded? In short, are we losing the ability to hope, to envisage the future as a place where it will be good to be, not just for those who are lucky enough to have the choice in such matters but also for those who struggle to make ends meet and who are voiceless? If so, we really have reached the end of history where boredom and apathy are the chief enemies. We shall be easy meat for those who will exploit 'the mediatization of politics', the spin-doctors and image makers and those who practise what David Harvey caustically calls 'economics with mirrors'. We shall be 'inviting the bitter harvest of charismatic politics and ideological extremism'.[7]

As we come to the close of the century, then, there are huge tides running, questions about the use of technology, about the future of work, about the increasing social divisions within a world where, ironically, communication has never been easier, about the reduction of everything and everyone to mere 'products', about the future of our cities and of nation-statehood. There are far-reaching anxieties about what George Steiner calls 'our unnerved culture'.[8] That is why I want to employ the metaphor of the surfer in a hopeful way.

After all, consider what the surfer is doing. One type of surfer is using a fairly frail craft to catch the next wave in seas which often are rough and which always must be exhilarating. She is driven forward at breakneck speed by waters of immense power. Another, the wind-surfer, uses a sail to catch the wind. Whether the water is shallow or deep does not seem to matter. Direction is the important thing, the angle of the sail against the wind. For both, timing, balance and nerve are essential. You could say that surfers are good at coping with change. They are also in an organic relationship with their world. In their best moments they must have a sense of being united with the elements. When people are coming to doubt their old relationship with the world around them, based on mastery, exploitation and power, to be in tune with nature, more at ease with our environment, may not be a bad thing.

I sense that many people are surfing at the present moment; surfing to keep their lives together in the face of immense waves of change that affect relationships, work, homes, values, sympathies and self-understanding. Merely to maintain their balance and to keep a sense of direction is a huge achievement and demands great nerve. True enough, there are some who surf the latest wave purely for selfish advantage and private gain. If that were the whole story, the only possible response would be despair.

However, we are not short of people who want to apply themselves to questions about the future, who care about the community of human beings, who will insist on more than a meagre safety net of social welfare, who believe in the morality of taxes, who value social and cultural diversity, who refuse to accept that human life will ever be reducible simply to economics, who resist the notion that the earth is a dustbin but who wish to use technology for its best purposes. I want to keep faith with them, their visions and their ability to find solutions for the world's problems and I believe the Christian Church should keep faith with them too. Sometimes it will all seem like surfing, skimming through successive waves of change with not too many of the resources that were available to previous generations. There will be repeated calls to take up old certainties that worked in another world but are inadequate for the Land of Unlikeness, which will either be an exhilarating place to be or an extremely frightening one. We constantly need to teach each other how to keep faith and perhaps we shall learn to do rather more than survive in what some of our forebears would regard as a rather thin atmosphere.

The response to the uncertainties with which we have to live in the modern world has frequently been a call 'to return' – return to traditional standards, to family values, to basics, to God even. The implication is obvious. The world, society, people have been getting away from a norm which previous generations have found valuable. The only way is back. I do not regard that as a worthy option for a Christian Church that has at its heart a belief in the constant presence of God in and through the world and humanity, both to re-create and to redeem. A belief like that both affirms the present moment and this world of experience, rather than some other one, and at the same time contains the seeds of hopefulness for the future.

I do not at all ignore the past and all that is of value in it; quite the contrary is the case. That is why I began with the past rather than the present in the first chapter. History situates us, but it should not anchor us in the past no matter how great are the challenges or even the horrors of the present. As Herbert Butterfield has said, 'it is never permitted to a Christian to despair of Providence'.9 The great offer of Christianity is the setting of human life within a continuum of past, present and future. Its reference point is rooted in history but its main thrust is always forwards. That is why the notion of progress in human society and knowledge took root within countries steeped in the Jewish-Christian tradition and why, despite all its failings which are in reality our failings, we must not abandon it now.

Therefore, I want to stay with a generation of surfers coping with difficult questions about God and redemption and the sort of society that will embody the values that Jesus taught, at precisely the time when everything around them is in a state of flux and when, amongst the other alternatives on offer, are nihilistic despair and fundamentalisms of many kinds. What will be asked of them is the ability to deal positively with change and to encourage other people not to be afraid of it; to keep their balance and nerve when competing demands are made upon them by society at large; to keep a sense of direction in the difficult moral decisions that new knowledge will require; and to do all this in conversation, in partnership, with others who share similar goals but perhaps without a shared faith. What sort of Christian community might assist them?

3. A common place

Bear with me while I try to draw together, to weave together, four separate strands into a *common place*.

1.   In his 1995 Reith Lectures the architect Richard Rogers, took as his theme 'Learning to Live with the City'. He drew on the distinction made by the American political theorist, Michael Walzer, between 'single-minded' and 'open-minded' spaces. The residential suburb, the car park, the business district are 'single-minded spaces'; the busy square, the lively street, the market, the park are 'open-minded spaces'. This distinction permeated much of what Richard Rogers had to say about living with the city of the next century. In his final lecture, he described how he and his partner entered, and lost, a competition to design the National Gallery's extension in London. As they surveyed the site they found that it held the key to unlocking the isolation of Trafalgar Square 'once the heart of Empire, now a polluted tourist trap encircled by traffic'. They suggested an open flight of public stairs from

Leicester Square down to Trafalgar Square, passing straight through their new building, the Gallery's extension, connecting with Trafalgar Square via a generous galleria, beneath the road. 'Two independent, but crucial, public places were physically woven together by a relatively small building.'10

That is a suggestive concept – a gallery, a public staircase, a relatively small building linking two public places – 'open-minded space' rather than 'single-minded space'. It speaks of movement, accessibility, linking together things which otherwise are separate. All of that sometimes comes in small packages.

2.   Elisabeth Schüssler Fiorenza follows a similar route as she develops the concept of the ekklesia of women as 'bounded open space', bounded because its limits are defined only by the different forms of struggle in which women and those dependent on women are engaged. Such an image for the piece of liberated space she envisages is not exclusive; it is available to all who wish to be there. Moreover it begins to redefine power as power for other people and not as power over other people. Within the bounded open space, relationships are changed. Hierarchy gives way to mutuality within a 'discipleship of equals'.11   For Fiorenza, table fellowship is important; it expresses all that is important in a meal shared and is a reminder of the common eating which both John Dominic Crossan and E. P. Sanders, from their different perspectives, take to be such a central part of the life and ministry of Jesus.12

Fiorenza's open space is a place of inclusiveness, of plurality, of giving and receiving around a common eating table.

3.   On my desk I have a hard copy of an article by Don Langham published in the *Computer-Mediated Communication Magazine*.13   It deals with the isolating and de-humanizing effects of communication through electronic media and begins with Socrates' condemnation of writing as the earliest protest in Western history at the dehumanizing effects of 'modern' technology! Langham recalls how important a sense of place is, a shared environment be it a room or a park, which can be the context for human communication.   Socrates criticized writing because it got in the way of speech between human beings in much the same way as critics speak of the isolating experience of computers.   Now computer communication is much more speedy and immediate than the written or printed page and, what is more, it is now becoming possible to create 'virtual' structures within the process in which those who communicate can be 'present' to one another in a way that is impossible in a telephone call or in the passivity of watching

television. A virtual structure might enable the communicators 'to be' in a library co-operating in the same research. Anyone who has talked to dedicated users of the Internet will have heard about virtual communities. Langham is reporting on research which will take us much further, with the possibility of providing 'the sort of structured environment needed for the "common place" of civilized society.'

With such an environment we are truly in the Land of Unlikeness. It suggests a new way in which human beings can be present to one another, and working with one another, across huge geographical and cultural divides and with almost the immediacy of speech.

4.   And finally there is the quantum society envisaged by Oxford Brookes' physicist and philosopher, Danah Zohar. The underlying theme of her work is that we have reached a point when new thinking is needed in how we understand our lives and our relationship to the natural world and to one another.   Once human beings perceived everything in a more or less harmonious relationship under God. That was succeeded by a mechanistic vision in which people clashed against one another like atoms in a chaotic fashion and needed to be subdued by force or social contract. Now we have an increasingly exhausted materialist individualism. For her, the 'wave-particle dualism' of quantum reality provides a new vision for human beings in society. Particles are individuals, located in a particular time and place. Waves, however, spread out across time and space; they overlap and combine to form new realities. Quantum reality can be particle-like and wave-like at the same time. A quantum view of society enables us to see how individuals derive their being within the whole, within creative relationships. What is true of individuals is also true of groups:

> There is not just 'my group' and 'your group' but the emergent society, the 'dance', in which all groups discover and explore and create themselves as they share their public space. That dance is the source of their common score, their consensus.[14]

Does that mean that, within a quantum society, everything is reduced to a common denominator? Is that what is meant by consensus? By no means:

> Inside me, inside each one of us, there is an infinite range of potential selves waiting to be evoked through relationship to others. The other is my opportunity, my necessity for growth. The otherness of the other, his or her difference, is a possibility sleeping within myself. I need the Muslim to be a Muslim, the Christian to be a Christian, the Jew to be a Jew. I need to be me, to hold my values, and I need you to hold yours. On a quantum understanding of the phrase, agreeing to disagree is agreeing upon something very fundamental indeed. That is the agreement upon which we can build our pluralistic consensus.[15]

Here is a view of a common place founded on great generosity and largeness of spirit. It carries with it a view that truth is not just multi-faceted – it all depends upon where you are standing – but that there may actually be more than one truth co-existing side by side which can achieve a harmony-in-relationship without being compromised.

These four perspectives on a shared place or space (they are not quite the same thing) offer us a new way of looking at the Christian community. They represent four different visions about what it means truly to be human beings at this particular moment in our history. If it is wise, the Christian Church will not be defensive, or too proud to learn from others what its vocation is to be. Neither will it be too imperialistic, acting as though it alone has the answers and that other people's views are always inadequate until they have been scrutinized and validated by us. Increasingly we will all need partners in our work. The sort of partnership which the Christian community as a common place would offer us would, among other things, provide for:

- difference without division
- plurality without indifference
- truth without threat
- realism without despair.

Furthermore, the idea of the Christian community as a common place provides a new perspective in which the different denominations might discover their greater unity. Mostly Christian unity conversations have been concerned with finding agreed statements in practice and doctrine which provide enough common ground on which to build. That has proved an unsatisfactory approach, probably because it is too static. It implies that the differences are obstacles that have to be surmounted, divisions that have to be healed. Of course, there are divisions that need healing but that has as much to do with attitude as belief. That is why we need to discover the quantum approach. Being what we are matters, being true to ourselves if you like, but this is not seen to be an obstacle so much as something to be celebrated by finding a common place in which we can work together.

And who knows but that this might represent a way by which we shall increasingly be able to work with and alongside other faith communities and also with the myriad separate communities that make up the complexity of our society. Can the church be seen to be, in the words of Dr. Joseph Cassidy of Southampton's La Sainte Union College, 'a community of communities', offering a common place, an 'open-minded space', without demands, for other communities of interest each seeking to articulate what Edward Schillebeeckx called 'the cry for the humane'?[16]

4.   A church of the common place

What will be the characteristics of a church of the common place, a church which is appropriate to the opportunities and challenges of the sort of world which I have been describing?

1.   It will be a place for those who believe that creation and redemption are inextricably bound together and who struggle to understand the God who is revealed to them within this tension. By creation I do not mean creationism, the doctrine that God literally made the world by divine command and evolution never happened. By creation I mean that all the laws of the natural world, which have given and are giving us life, and which are open to the inquiring human mind, are God's laws. Those laws are the ways by which God, whose name and nature is love, has accepted self-limitation in the continuing process of creation. As far as we know, human beings are alone in being able to choose between right and wrong. God's way of redemption is our hope that the purposes of creation shall not be frustrated by human waywardness. More than that, it is the hope that in the end all that is will be brought to completion and wholeness in the patient unfolding of God's love. The church of the common place will struggle to keep the tension between

creation and redemption which is true to the Jewish-Christian biblical tradition because we believe that all that is has its life in God.

2.   The church of the twenty-first century will understand that the world is getting smaller and bigger – at the same time. Smaller in the sense that there is virtually nowhere beyond the reach of a package holiday; smaller in that teleworkers in a remote Scottish island input material from journals flown over to them from the States and then send their work back to their database editor in California via the Internet; smaller in the sense that many ecological issues are not global but intensely local; and bigger in the sense that there is so much more of it, and it is far more complex than we ever realized – just look at the vast numbers of special interest magazines now available on the newsagent's shelves, made possible by desktop publishing and all catering for an increasing number of individuals; bigger in the sense that a global perspective is increasingly demanded by employers, with life-time learning and languages a high priority.

It will be perfectly possible for churches to offer a back-to-the-cradle experience, a highly appealing strategy as the advertising industry knows only too well. Is that, however really how the Christian Church sees its purpose? For generations, we have had a dynamic of world mission. We need now to take all that is best and creative about that experience to enable people to have a global perspective which embraces the justice, peace and integrity of creation as its major goals.

3.   That same perspective will impel the church of the common place to look for partners. I suspect that the very complexity of the world will lead us in this direction. I call it the church of the open door. In a world where nations and businesses look for alliances either for protective or predatory purposes, why should not the church look for partnerships in the cause of good? We do already, of course, but often with the sense that it is second best. The proper work is elsewhere, we like to think. However, in every locality there are partnerships to be forged, with people of faith and of no faith, which not only build up a sense of belonging but which are pointers to the generosity of God.

4.   All of which leads to a church which seeks to be in a creative relationship with 'the world'. I hesitate to use that expression because it is so capable of misunderstanding. The church has a reputation for being unworldly if not other-worldly. Undeniably there is a strain in the biblical record which is highly wary of *the world*. Those texts need to be handled sensitively,

however, and with a sense of perspective, a perspective that once again holds together creation and redemption. In a brilliant book re-visioning Christian mission in a series of startling metaphors, Donald Messer puts his finger on the problem:

> Too many local churches function with the old foreign mission compound mentality. Their structure recalls a bygone era and a different group of people. They see their local neighbourhoods as alien places, full of folk who think and act differently, sing unusual music, eat exotic foods, and share a hostile culture. Ironically, some of these congregations continue to support missionaries in distant countries, but they treat their neighbours as nonpersons. These congregations need to learn from the experience of missionaries and to begin to understand and translate the language and culture of their neighbourhoods.[17]

5. A church of the common place will embrace new knowledge gladly, will reflect on it critically and celebrate those who use it wisely. There is nothing to be gained from obscurantism or from suspicion. Neither should we leap too soon to moralize about new knowledge before understanding it. This will be particularly the case in the burgeoning field of genetics and in the exploration of human consciousness, both of which so directly affect us all. Therefore, we need to encourage the scientists amongst us not to be too easily silenced by the language of faith which the church uses in its hymns and prayers, and which sometimes suggests a pre-modern age. Neither should they be discouraged from saying to us, 'This is how it is, difficult though it may be for you to come to terms with.' The alternative is a discreet silence and a widening gap between faith and reality.

6. A church which tries to minister to people living in the kind of portfolio world described so vividly by Charles Handy and others (see chapter two), has an unsuspected human resource who, if they reflected on the nature of their own work, would realize that they already have a great deal of experience of the kind of world that most people are now entering in their working lives. At this point I am well aware of the dangers both of generalization and prediction. Both can so easily be wide of the mark.

Let us suppose, however, that the prophets are correct and a whole swathe of work becomes more and more individualized: people working for themselves, at home, networking, on short contracts, meeting colleagues not in the office but in homes or other suitable meeting places, finding difficulty in contacting people, having a telephone ring at home at all hours or work encroaching on meals or family time, experiencing the loneliness of working alone, or its sense of freedom or responsibility, learning self-motivation and how to set boundaries between work and personal time.

What is the human resource that the church has to offer to people like these? Well, its ministers and clergy have mostly been working like that for years. The irony is that they have been under-valuing themselves and their work precisely because they do not go to the office, because they do not appear to be professional, because they know the frustration of not being certain of contacting the people they need to in order to have the satisfaction of completing that day's work. Ministers and clergy, therefore, need to reassess their work and their own sense of ministry, to be helped to grow a new sense of confidence in the value of what they are doing, because they have much to offer to those in their communities who are experiencing the vulnerability and challenge of fragmented patterns of working.

7.   Finally, the church for a generation of surfers will discover, or perhaps recover, the real place of the sermon in its common life. At first sight, that sounds completely incongruous. Preaching does not have a very good image, but that is precisely the point. Preaching has become associated with a rhetorical style which tells you what you have to do or believe and where you have gone wrong. As such, it is deeply suspect.

Part of the problem has to do with the belief that preaching is proclamation. This stems from the understanding that in the Acts of the Apostles, the disciples proclaimed the central events of the saving gospel of God in a quite direct way – Jesus, who was crucified, God raised from the dead; therefore, repent of your sins and be baptized, all of you! What we forget is that the apostolic preaching was almost always concluded with a question from the audience, 'Therefore, what shall we do?' The message was understood because it set up the beginnings of a conversation in the mind of the hearer which had to be taken further. The act of preaching included both the proclamation and the response, 'We understand that what you are saying applies to us. Now show us how to respond.'

When I say, therefore, that we need to recover the proper place of the sermon in our common life, I mean that we can reclaim preaching as conversation, a way of speaking about God which sets up a stream of consciousness amongst the hearers, both individually and corporately, in which all share. The sermon then becomes a true conversation between preacher and hearers, even though only one of them is speaking!

The sermon as conversation is really but a return to the roots of the word itself. More than once, Cicero contrasted *sermo* with *oratio* where the context is usually of conversation. The word we use for the study of preaching, *homiletics*, comes from a Greek background in which 'being together' and 'conversing together' are frequently indicated.[18] What, over many centuries of tradition, has come to be regarded as a one-person exposition of truth, in reality has its roots in the same fertile soil of conversation which, I have come to believe, is now the appropriate way of doing theology. It is not surprising, therefore, that there is a renewed interest in rhetoric amongst postmodernist writers where engagement with the issues and persuasion of an audience are the order of the day. Amongst Christian theologians who have studied the art of the sermon, Fred Craddock puts it at its simplest when he talks about the nod of recognition and the shock of recognition. The people are at home with the sermon just as the people were at home with the parables and stories which Jesus told. They nod their assent and mentally say, 'That's right!' In the very familiarity of the sermon's message, in the tacit conversation between preacher and people, there is the realization that what is being said 'applies, is God's word to me' – the shock of recognition. As Craddock himself has it, the preacher is not saying what the people want to hear; she or he is saying what the people would want to say if they were the preacher.[19]

5. A highway shall be there

Finally, will there still be a place for all that the community of faith represents? Having brought us to the End of History, Francis Fukuyama has turned his attention to the importance of trust within national economies. It is civil society that builds trust, he says. Civil society is a complex mixture of businesses, voluntary associations, educational institutions, clubs, unions, media, charities and churches. The nurturing of people's lives through this intricate web of relationships all adds up to what he calls 'social capital', which it is easier to dissipate than to produce.[20] This is not unrelated to what I take to be the most serious challenge that lies ahead of us, our ability to maintain the reality of human beings living in society with a sense of obligation and mutuality.

There are increasing pressures that pull us apart. We have noticed some of them; the fragmentation of working patterns into smaller units, the narrower horizons of individualism – what is good and right for me and my family – the insistence on rights, which often leads to single issue politics, the tendency, in the face of violence, menace and uncertain values, to live behind security fences. There is a nagging anxiety that the new technology which ought to bring us all much closer together and open up a way for greater inter-dependence and communication, might actually lead to increasing isolation. Are we being sold another form of reality which will turn out in reality, virtual or not, to be fantasy? Will the ultimate division in a technologically rich world be the opting out by communities of the wealthy across the world, controlling their wealth digitally and fortifying their homes with electronic hardware and private police forces against the depredations of the have-nots at their gates?

But we have also seen that other, more hopeful values are on offer, with a larger vision of what it is to be a human being. The shape of morality is changing. For a generation of younger people morality now includes a care for the planet; racism and sexism are becoming unacceptable to most thinking people although both still flourish in places and will die hard. University computer departments look closely at the ethics of their subject; business schools offer courses on ethics and leadership; in the finance world, green investments are increasingly seen as a profitable option. All of this is not the preserve of Christianity, but it is the sort of territory upon which faith has always operated. It is not the whole of faith, but it will be seen by many as its cutting edge; faith will want to say more, but it cannot say less. It will best communicate its essence not from the exclusivist position of fundamentalism but as a community of faith which offers a common place to all, a place which nurtures a critical, contemporary Christianity. I outlined what I mean by a critical, contemporary Christianity in chapter three. No doubt that can be improved upon, but here again are its central features as I understand them:

> – a commitment to interpret the Christian understanding of God, rooted as it is in a shared biblical tradition, at the heart of which is the creative presence and redeeming love of God which for Christian people is focused in Jesus Christ;

> – a decision to measure the tradition of faith as it has been given us against the demands of the present day, at the inter-

section of which we discover what it is for us to keep faith, both in our believing and in our living;

–   its manner is one of excitement and humility. We are in Küng's words 'open to learn and ready to discuss' but 'rooted in the Christian tradition';[21]

–   it is truly ecumenical and set against the widest horizons;

–   it is people-centred by which I mean that:

    –   being human has a value that is not reducible simply to biological or any other descriptions,

    –   we have the means of discovering that which makes for our peace and healing,

    –   we have within us a deep-laid sense of obligation to others.

The community of faith as a common place for all has another role to play, particularly for a surfing generation working hard to deal with the present and with half an eye on what will become of us. It will safeguard the memory. Richard Hoggart may well be right in saying that we are a generation of people who have no sense of a 'usable past'. Václav Havel says that one of the first things that their old communist masters did was to separate the people from the 'disquieting dimension of history': 'In our own country, too, one has the impression that for some time there has been no history. Slowly but surely we are losing the sense of time.'[22] By the same token I recently heard someone talking about the vast number of early retirements in industry nowadays as 'the loss of the company's memory'.

Therefore, just as the quiet inhabitants of a monastery, in their cycle of worship and meditation, safeguard the prayers of the likes of you and me who are enmeshed in the busy world, just as in the societies of old the grand-mothers and grandfathers guarded the people's history, so the community of faith, which is the common place, will safeguard memory on behalf of a generation for whom the past is another country. And who knows when the past will become usable again? This is the truth of Christianity's central act of worship, 'That the Lord Jesus, on the night when . . .'

One of the tantalizing themes in the biblical record is the interplay between the place and the way. It begins in the Land between the Two Rivers in the twelfth chapter of Genesis with Abram and Sarai being called to go to another land that God will show them. When, a few chapters later, they discover the place, they do not settle it; they travel through it. The story moves on a few hundred years until Isaiah declares there is a highway through dry land from which fools and sinners are excluded, but along which the blind, the dumb, the lame and the deaf will sing and dance. When we reach the very last pages of the Book of Revelation the theme is still being played out but now the land has become a city. Throughout the whole of the story, you are never quite sure whether what you have been searching for is a land, or a city, or whether it is *God*.

In the Christian tradition the guide is Christ – the way, the truth, the life – although we have tended to concentrate overmuch on the small English word 'the', which has become a mark of exclusiveness, especially in how we pronounce the whole phrase. And we have missed the sheer pace, the breath-taking vitality of the great biblical and Johannine ideas of Way, Truth and Life, each of which is a hidden compendium of movement and discovery. We move along the way; the Holy Spirit leads us into more truth; life is water bubbling up out of the ground and flowing freely. The direction is always forward, always pressing onwards.

The Jewish tradition in the Old Testament gave God many descriptions but its characteristic expression, the one that sums up all the rest, is 'the living God'. It marked out the true God from the idols; it was the living God who was the source of life to all creatures and who patiently watched over creation. When the Jewish St. Paul went to the city of Athens (Acts 17) to engage its philosophers in a conversation about God, he quoted one of their own poets, 'In him we live and move and have our being.' It is, I believe, the living God who best fits the circumstances in which we find ourselves at the end of one century and on the verge of another, when amongst all the questions that confront us, there are those which ask if we have the spiritual resources to cope with all that we now know, and whether or not we have the moral capacity, with all the diversity of the human race, to live well together.

Keeping faith with the living God will mean that constantly we will need to hold together an understanding of what we are saying by *creation* and *redemption*. The Christian understanding of the patient, hidden, creating work of God will not stand still, particularly when one realizes that somewhere out there in the fresh century there will probably be some new revolutionary thing, some new discovery, some new branch of learning as completely unpredicted as was information technology just a few decades ago. We know enough to realize that though 'love's redeeming work is done', there is always more work to be done. There will be no utopias, just the costly work of God who will not let the creation go, redeeming the waste of life, renewing the earth through the Spirit and holding all things together in Christ.

NOTES

TITLE PAGES

Václav Havel, *Toward a Civil Society, Selected Speeches and Writings*, 1990-1994, Lidove Noviny Publishing House, Prague, p. 307.

W. H. Auden, from 'Flight into Egypt', *Collected Poems* Faber and Faber Ltd.

INTRODUCTION

p. 1   1.   John F. Haught, *Science and Religion*, Paulist Press 1996.

p. 2   2.   Richard Hoggart, *The Way We Live Now*, Chatto and Windus 1995. His opening sentence is: 'This is a surf-riding phase in British life.'

1. THE TWENTIETH CENTURY – ANOTHER LOOK

p. 4   1.   John C. Heenan, *Not The Whole Truth*, Hodder 1973, p.17.

p. 5   2.   Adrian Desmond and James Moore, *Darwin*, Penguin 1992, p.160.

p. 5   3.   Tennyson, *Works*, p.649.

p. 6   4.   Desmond and Moore, p.488.

p. 7   5.   John A. T. Robinson, *Honest To God*, SCM Press 1963, p.7.

p. 7   6.   Robinson, p.41.

p. 7   7.   Robinson, p.139.

p. 9   8.   Michael Polanyi, *Personal Knowledge*, University of Chicago Press, 1974 (first published 1958) p.17.

p. 10   9.   H. Richard Niebuhr, *Christ and Culture*, Faber and Faber Ltd 1952, p.46.

p. 10   10.   Hans Küng, *Theology for the Third Millennium*, HarperCollins 1991, p.1.

p. 11   11.   Simon Callow, 'In times of plague and pestilence', *The Observer*, 26.9.93.

p. 11   12.   Friedrich Nietzsche, *Thus Spoke Zarathustra*, Penguin 1969, p.59.

p. 12   13.   Linda Grant, 'Knee-Benders for the truth', *The Guardian*, 11.4.96.

p. 13   14.   Charles Handy, *The Empty Raincoat*, Hutchinson 1994, p.1. See also *The Age of Unreason*.

2. END OF CENTURY

p. 14   1.   T. S. Eliot, from 'East Coker', *Four Quartets, Collected Poems 1909-1962*, Faber and Faber Ltd 1974, p.196.

p. 15   2.   Donald English, *Into the Twenty-First Century*, Methodist Church Home Mission

p. 17   3.   *Hymns & Psalms* 339, The Methodist Publishing House 1983.

p. 18   4.   Danah Zohar, *The Quantum Self*, Flamingo 1991, p.2. See also *The Quantum Society*, Flamingo 1994.

p. 19   5.   John Polkinghorne, *Serious Talk*, SCM Press 1996, p.17.

p. 19   6.   Bruce Mazlish, *The Fourth Discontinuity*, Yale 1993. Mazlish says that the first supposed discontinuity to be disposed of was that between the earth and the rest of the solar system (Copernicus); the second, between human beings and the natural world (Darwin); the third between our conscious and unconscious selves (Freud).

p. 19   7.   David C. Thomasma, *Human Life in the Balance*, Westminster/John Knox Press 1990, p.60.

p. 19   8.   Nicholas Negroponte, *Being Digital*, p.4. Reproduced by permission of Hodder & Stoughton 1995.

p. 20   9.   Douglas Hague, 'Lost on the Superhighway', *The Times*.

p. 20   10.   For a discussion on the importance of perspective for renaissance map-making, see David Harvey, *The Condition of Postmodernity*, p.245ff.

p. 21   11.   Negroponte p.165.

p. 22   12.   Francis Fukuyama, *Trust. The Social Virtues and the Creation of Prosperity*, Hamish Hamilton 1995, p.256.

p. 22   13.   'The world that changed the machine', *The Economist*, 30.3.96

p. 22   14.   Hamish McRae, *The World in 2020*, HarperCollins 1995, p.67.

p. 23   15.   Robin Gill, *The Myth of the Empty Church*, SPCK 1993.

p. 24   16.   Walter Rauschenbusch, *Christianity and the Social Crisis*, edited by Robert Graves, Harper Torchbooks 1964, originally published in 1907 by The Macmillan Company.

p. 24   17.   Charles Handy p.176-7.

p. 25   18.   E. R. Wickham, *Church and People in an Industrial City*, Lutterworth Press 1962 p.15.

p. 25   19.   Elaine Showalter, *Sexual Anarchy: Gender and Culture at the Fin de Siècle*, Bloomsbury 1991, p.17.

p. 25   20.   Elisabeth Schüssler Fiorenza, *In Memory of Her*, SCM Press 1983.

p. 26   21.   Virginia Woolf, *A Room of One's Own*, Harcourt 1929 p.68. Quoted by Rebecca S. Chopp in *The Power to Speak; Feminism, Language, God*, Crossroads N.Y. 1989, p.2.

p. 27   22.   McRae, p.277.

p. 28   23.   Tony Robinson, 'I still find the Bible narrative inspiring', *The Sunday Telegraph* 15.10.95.

3. FUTURE CHOICES

p. 29   1.   Francis Fukuyama, *The End of History and the Last Man*, Penguin 1992, p.335f.

p. 30   2.   Paul Rabinov, *Space, Knowledge and Power*, in *The Foucault Reader*, Penguin 1984, p.249.

p. 30   3.   Ernest Gellner, *Postmodernism, Reason and Religion*, Routledge 1992, p.85.

p. 31   4.   Susan Howatch, *Ultimate Prizes*, HarperCollins 1993, p.146.

p. 31   5.   Jim Wallis, *The Soul of Politics,* Fount 1995, p xi.

p. 31   6.   Hal Foster, *Postmodern Culture*, Pluto Press 1983, p.ix

p. 32   7.   Rabinov, p.211.

p. 32   8.   Clive Marsh, *Postmodernism: What is it, and does it matter?* Epworth Review, May 1994 pp.44ff.

p. 33   9.   Sallie McFague, *Models of God*, Fortress 1987, p.182.

p. 33   10.   David Harvey, p.355.

p. 34   11.   Patricia Waugh, *Postmodernism: A Reader*, Edward Arnold 1992, p.9.

p. 34   12.   *People and the New World of Work*, St. George's House, Windsor. 1995, p.13.

p. 35   13.   Julie Burchill, 'The religion of the Me Generation', *The Sunday Times* 15.10.95.

p. 36   14.   Ernest Gellner, p.58.

p. 36   15.   Alvin Toffler, *Future Shock*, Pan Books 1971, p.341-346.

p. 37   16.   Terry Eagleton, *Ideology,* Verso 1991, p.4.

p. 38   17.   Stephen Toulmin, *Cosmopolis*, University of Chicago 1990, p.183.

p. 38   18.   Stephen Toulmin, *The 17th Century Counter-Renaissance,* in *Cosmopolis* p.45ff.

p. 39   19.   Stephen Toulmin, p.179.

p. 39   20.   Stephen Toulmin, p.200f.

p. 39   21.   Methodist Faith and Order Committee Report, *Called to Love and Praise* 1995, paragraphs 2.1.1. and 2.1.2.

p. 40   22.   Hans Küng and David Tracy, *Paradigm Change in Theology*, T. & T. Clark 1989, p.440.

p. 40   23.   Hamish McRae, p.176.

p. 41   24.   Richard Rogers, The 1995 Reith Lectures, 'Learning to Live with the City', *The Independent*, 13.2.95. © Newspaper Publishing plc.

p. 41   25.   Eric Hobsbawm, *Age of Extremes, The Short Twentieth Century 1914-1991*, Michael Joseph 1994, p.4.

p.41   26.   Eric Hobsbawm, p.584.

4. CONVERSATION

p. 44   1.   Charles Handy, *Understanding Organizations*.

p. 46   2.   David Tracy, *Plurality and Ambiguity*, SCM 1987, p.29.

p. 47   3.   Václav Havel, *Toward a Civil Society, Selected Speeches and Writings*, 1990-1994, Lidove Noviny Publishing House, Prague, p.231.

p. 48   4.   James Dunn, *Unity and Diversity in the New Testament*, SCM Press 1977.

p. 48   5.   John Wesley, *Forty-Four Sermons, No.33, A Caution against Bigotry*.

p. 49   6.   Hans Küng and David Tracy, *Paradigm Change in Theology*, p.445.

p. 50   7.   Hans Küng and David Tracy, p.469.

p. 52   8.   Léon-E. Halkin, *Erasmus, A Critical Biography*, Blackwell, p.296.

p. 52   9.   Hamish McRae, p.267.

p. 52   10.   Will Hutton, *The State We're In*, Jonathan Cape 1995, p.290.

p. 52   11.   Eric Hobsbawm, p.567.

5. ARE WE GETTING AHEAD OF GOD?

p. 53   1.   Alan Jenkins, 'To love, honour and betray', *GQ* April 1995.

p. 56   2.   'Afterwards', Thomas Hardy, from *The Complete Poems*, Papermac/Macmillan

p. 56   3.   Mervyn Willshaw, *What on earth is God doing?* A paper written for the Methodist Apologetics Group.

p. 56   4.   John Macquarrie, *Paths in Spirituality*, SCM Press 1972, p.28.

p. 57   5.   Nicholas Negroponte, *Being Digital*, p.15.

p. 59   6   Richard Dawkins, *The Blind Watchmaker*, Penguin 1988, p.5.

p. 59   7.   Paul Davies, *The Edge of Infinity*, Penguin 1994, p.171.

p. 60   8.   Richard Dawkins, p.43.

p. 60   9.   p.139.

p. 60   10.   p.148.

p. 60   11.   p.163.

p. 61   12.   p.165.

p. 62   13.   Steve Jones, *The Language of the Genes*, Flamingo 1994, p.xi.

p. 63   14.   Philippians 2:7.

p. 63   15.   *Hymns & Psalms* 109. See also 101 and 216.

p. 63   16.   Richard Dawkins, *River out of Eden*.

p. 65   17.   *The Independent*, January 1995.

p. 66   18.   *The Independent*, 17.1.96

6. 'NOTHING IS BEYOND REDEMPTION'

p. 67   1.   Sebastian Faulks, *Birdsong*, Vintage 1994, p.348.

p. 68   2.   E. Annie Proulx, *The Shipping News*, Fourth Estate 1993, p.1.

p. 69   3.   David Gutterson, *Snow Falling on Cedars*, Bloomsbury 1995.

p. 69   4.   John Updike, *Rabbit at Rest*, Penguin 1991, p.512.
Also – *Rabbit, Run*, (1964). *Rabbit Redux*, (1973), *Rabbit is Rich*,
(1982)

p. 69   5.   Alan Richardson, *A Theological Word Book of the Bible*,
SCM Press 1957.

p. 70   6.   Peter Berger, *A Rumour of Angels*, Penguin 1970, p.70.

p. 70   7.   Norman Maclean, *A River Runs Through It*, Picador 1993, p.104.

p. 71   8.   C. G. Jung, *Memories, Dreams, Reflections*, Fontana Press 1995, p.138.

p. 71   9.   Irenaeus, *Adversus Haereses 5*, quoted in J. N. D. Kelley, *Early
Christian Doctrines*, A. & C. Black 1958, p.172.

p. 72   10.   See James Dunn's *Christology in the Making*, SCM Press 1980/89, for
a fuller discussion of Adam and Christ in Paul's thinking, p.98ff.

p. 72   11.   Steve Jones, *The Language of the Genes*, Flamingo 1993, p.3.

p. 72   12.   Timothy Gorringe, *Redeeming Time*, Darton, Longman & Todd 1986,
p.52.

p. 73   13.   Sigmund Freud, *Art and Literature*, Penguin 1990, p.249ff.

p. 75   14.   Mary Grey, *Redeeming the Dream*, SPCK 1989, p.124.

p. 75   15.   Robert F. Wearmouth, *The Social and Political Influence of Methodism
in the Twentieth Century*, Epworth Press 1957, p.220.

p. 76   16.   Jim Wallis, *The Soul of Politics*, Fount 1994, p.xix.

p. 77   17.   David Clark, *Lay Vocation – The Call to Becoming Persons*, (*The
Human City Initiative*) Christians in Public Life Programme, Position
Paper F10.

p. 77   18.   William Wordsworth, *The World is too much with us.*

p. 78   19.   Frances Young, *Can These Dry Bones Live?* SCM Press 1982, p.70.

p. 79   20.   For a full discussion of the language of sacrifice, see Frances Young (p.65ff) and Timothy Gorringe, *Redeeming Time*, Darton, Longman & Todd 1986, p.46ff

7. THE LAND OF UNLIKENESS

p. 81   1.   Deyan Sudjic, *The 100 Mile City*, Flamingo 1993.

p. 81   2.   Will Hutton, p.325.

p. 81   3.   Hamish McRae, p.205.

p. 82   4.   Jon Swain, *The Sunday Times* 28.1.96.

p. 83   5.   Richard Hoggart, p.331.

p. 83   6.   Richard Hoggart, p.325.

p. 84   7.   David Harvey, p.329, 337.

p. 84   8.   George Steiner, 'No Passion Spent', *Essays 1978-1996*, Faber & Faber Ltd 1996 p. ix.

p. 86   9.   Herbert Butterfield, *God in History*, in C.T. McIntire's *Writings on Christianity and History*, OUP 1975, p.13.

p. 87   10.   The 1995 Reith Lectures, 'Learning to Live with the City', *The Independent* 27.2.95. © Newspaper Publishing plc

p. 87   11.   Elisabeth Schüssler Fiorenza, *Discipleship of Equals*, SCM Press 1993, p.333ff.

p. 87   12.   John Dominic Crossan, *The Historical Jesus*, T. & T. Clark 1991, p.402.

        E. P. Sanders, *Jesus and Judaism*, SCM Press 1985, p.208.

p. 87   13.   Don Langham, 'The Common Place MOO: Orality and Literacy in Virtual Reality', *Computer-Mediated Communication Magazine, Vol.1. No.3.* 1.7.94.

p. 88   14.   Danah Zohar, *The Quantum Society*, Flamingo 1994, p.276.

p. 89   15.   Danah Zohar, p.278.

p. 90   16.   Edward Schillebeeckx, The Role of History in what is called the New Paradigm. In Küng and Tracy, *Paradigm Change in Theology*, T. & T. Clark 1989, p.318.

p. 92   17.   Donald E. Messer, *A Conspiracy of Goodness*, Abingdon 1992, p.160.

p. 94   18.   I am grateful to Derek Long for this.

p. 94   19.   See Fred B. Craddock, *Overhearing the Gospel*, Abingdon 1978.

p. 94   20.   Francis Fukuyama, *Trust*, Hamish Hamilton 1995, p.362. See also Jeremy Rifkind in *The End of Work* (1996).

p. 96   21.   Hans Küng, *Paradigm Change in Theology*, p.440.

p. 96   22.   Václav Havel, *Dear Mr Husak,* in *Open Letters 1965-1990*, Faber and Faber Ltd 1991, p.73f.